GLOBALECTICS

The Wellek Library Lectures in Critical Theory

The Wellek Library Lectures in Critical Theory
are given annually at the University of California, Irvine,
under the auspices of the Critical Theory Institute.
The following lectures were given in May 2010.

The Critical Theory Institute
Kavita Phillips, Director

GLOBALECTICS

THEORY AND THE POLITICS OF KNOWING

Ngũgĩ wa Thiong'o

Columbia University Press   *New York*

Columbia University Press
Publishers Since 1893
New York   Chichester, West Sussex
cup.columbia.edu
Copyright © 2012 Ngũgĩ wa Thiong'o
Paperback edition, 2014
All rights reserved

Library of Congress Cataloging-in-Publication Data
Ngugi wa Thiong'o, 1938–
Globalectics : theory and the politics of knowing / Ngugi wa Thiong'o.
p.   cm. — (The Wellek library lectures in critical theory)
Includes bibliographical references and index.
ISBN 978-0-231-15950-0 (cloth : alk. paper)
ISBN 978-0-231-15951-7 (pbk. : alk. paper)
ISBN 978-0-231-53075-0 (e-book)
1. Literature—History and criticism—Theory, etc.   2. Knowledge, Theory
of.   3. Literature and globalization.   4. African literature—Political
aspects.   5. Postcolonialism in literature.   I. Title.   II. Series: Wellek Library
lecture series at the University of California, Irvine.
PN441.N47 2012
801'.9—dc23
2011025562
∞
Columbia University Press books are printed on permanent and durable acid-free paper.
Printed in the United States of America
c 10 9 8 7 6 5 4 3 2
p 10 9 8 7 6 5 4 3 2 1

Cover image: Sokey Edorh, Les Gendarmes d'Afrique, 2006.
Collection: Newark Museum. Courtesy Skoto Gallery.
Photo credit: Newark Museum/Art Resource, NY.
Cover design: Milenda Nan Ok Lee

References to Internet Web sites (URLs) were accurate at the time of writing. Neither
the author nor Columbia University Press is responsible for URLs that may have
expired or changed since the manuscript was prepared.

*In memory of the late Henry Owuor Anyumba and for
Taban lo Liyong, fellow authors of the 1969 statement;
for all the members of the Department of Literature at Nairobi
who entered the debate with energy and creative suggestions;
and for all those who later extended the debate to include
the reorganization of literature in schools*

CONTENTS

ACKNOWLEDGMENTS

I celebrated my seventieth birthday at Irvine a couple of years ago with festivities organized by Gabriele Schwab, David Goldberg, and Ackbar Abbas. The event attracted a large number of faculty and students at Irvine and prompted generous comments from Angela Davis, Chancellor Michael Drake, and Zachary Muburi-Muita, the Kenyan ambassador to the United Nations, among others. The highlight was an unforgettable performance by Liu Sola, a Chinese composer and novelist, and Koffi Koko, a Ghanaian dancer, during which we witnessed two civilizations in dialogue with each other and the present, through a combination of sound, silence, motion, flute music, and drums. The celebrations reminded me that *ni mebwaga chumvi nyingi* (I have eaten a lot of salt), as we would say in Kiswahili, which means that I have earned the right to look back and tell tales of the past. It was not a coincidence that I published the first of my memoirs, *Dreams in a Time of War*, soon after. And now, the 2010 Wellek Library Lectures in Critical Theory.

I would like to thank the director of the Critical Theory Institute, Professor Kavita Phillips, for the invitation to give the lectures, for it afforded me an opportunity to look back on my involvement with literature as a novelist, theorist, and public intellectual over the last forty-eight years. This obviously includes my last eight years at UCI, where I have enjoyed creative interactions with my colleagues in the departments of Comparative Literature, English, and Drama, the Program of African American Studies, and the School of Humanities. The focus and direction of the lectures emerged out of exploratory talks with Professor Gaby Schwab, who encouraged me to look back on the theme of return that runs through my life and work. Even when she was away from the campus as a visiting professor at Arizona and Rutgers, she took the time to discuss and suggest useful sources. I gained a lot from Professor John H. Smith's lifelong study of Hegel. We had several arranged and impromptu discussions and he also went over some of the drafts with useful comments and suggestions. Professor Jane Newman, who showed great interest in the progress of these lectures, gave me tons of material on world literature. She also made useful comments on some of the drafts. Barbara Caldwell, my indefatigable assistant and researcher, carried out my daily requests for books and references with calm efficiency. Mukoma wa Ngugi kept on feeding me useful suggestions for readings and ways of approaching my subject. The final shape of the titles came after a very intense debate with Mukoma and his wife, Maureen. Professor Chris Wanjala was very helpful in unearthing material on the literature debate and the curriculum that followed the debate. In addition, he and Henry Chakava gave some useful information on Henry Owuor Anyumba. I am grateful for the support in material and information that I got from Lisa Ness Clark, administrator of the Critical Theory Institute.

I would like to thank many friends, including Peter Nazareth, Susie Tharu, Bahadur Tejani, Timothy J. Reiss, Patricia Penn Hilden, and Meena Alexander, who continually add to my global thinking. Professor Jennifer Wicke first set me on the path of consciously and specifically thinking about globalization and literature when she asked me and Christopher Miller to give a seminar on that theme at Yale in the mid-nineties. Some of my thinking on the globality of the postcolonial in chapter 3 has roots in that seminar and my four years at Yale as visiting professor of English and Comparative Literature, from 1989 to 1992. Professor Gayatri Spivak, whom I first met at the late Paul Engels's house in Iowa in 1966, continues to inspire with her immersion in languages—European, African, Asian, big and small—and her advocacy for the visibility of "the subaltern" languages in the Western academy.

It will be obvious to those who have followed my work since I came to Irvine in 2002 that the activities of the International Center for

Writing and Translation on global conversations among languages and cultures have impacted my thinking on the possibilities inherent in a give-and-take of language and culture contact on a global scale. I would like to thank members of the executive board; the late Jacques Derrida; Karen Lawrence; Wole Soyinka; Manthia Diawara; Dilek Dizdar; Bei Ling Huang; Tove Skutnabb-Kangas; Gayatri Spivak; Lawrence Venuti; Michael Wood; the former acting director, Dragan Kujundzic; the current director, Colette Labouff Atkinson; the managers, Chris Aschan and Lynh Tran; and all the members of the advisory boards as well as the benefactor of the center, Glenn Schaffer.

I would like to thank Professor Micere Mugo for sending me her book on orature and human rights and for many years of literary collaboration.

Last but not least, I would like to thank my family living with me at Irvine! I tried all the variations of the titles and openings on my wife, Njeeri, who bore all my groans with the response, "Just do it!" My son, Thiong'o, and daughter, Mumbi, were probably sick of hearing about the Welleks, even as I drove them to school, but they did not show it. Instead, they kept on asking me, with sympathy, if I had finished with Mr. Wellek.

Well, there's no way of finishing with René Wellek, for looking at all the luminous minds that have preceded me, and those that will follow, René Wellek continues to inspire different ways of reading literature and theory.

GLOBALECTICS

Riches of Poor Theory

Though other literary thinkers may have had a bigger impact on each of those who came of intellectual age in the early sixties, as I did as an undergraduate at Makerere (1959–60) and a graduate student at Leeds (1965–67), we could not have entirely escaped René Wellek's direct or indirect influence. In my case, I find a few other parallels. He came into English from Czech and German as I did from Gĩkũyũ and Kiswahili. He taught in the School of Slavonic and East European languages, now part of the University of London. My alma mater, Makerere, was part of the University of London, and, despite my campus being Kampala, Uganda, I actually hold a University of London degree. He taught at Iowa, eventually at Yale, a founder of its Comparative Literature Department. Iowa was the second campus, after New York University, that I visited when I first set foot in America in 1966 on the occasion of the International PEN Congress hosted by the PEN American Center, when Arthur Miller was the president of International PEN. Years later, as an exile, I found myself a visiting professor of English and comparative literature at Yale for four years (1989–92), before I moved to New York University as professor of English and Comparative Literature and holder of the Erich Maria Remarque Professorship of Languages. In 2002 I relocated to the University of California, Irvine, as Distinguished Professor of English and Comparative Literature and the founding director of the International Center for Writing and Translation (ICWT), where we engaged issues of translation—what we preferred to call conversation among languages and cultures. In a way this conversation among cultures, and literature in particular, was also the theme in Wellek and Warren's advocacy of comparativity in their book *Theory of Literature*, where they decry lack of contact between the students of different languages, stressing the "grotesque consequences when literary problems are discussed only with regard to views expressed in the particular language."[1] They were talking of European languages—mainly English, French, German, and Russian—but the sentiment could apply to other languages equally. At the International Center for Writing and Translation, we took our motto of "culture contact as oxygen" from Aimé Césaire's *Discourse on Colonialism*, where he writes "that whatever its own particular genius may be, a civilization that withdraws into itself atrophies; that for civilizations, exchange is oxygen."[2] The theme of culture contact through languages runs through these lectures.

Being a member of the Critical Theory Institute (CTI), my choice of subject and approach has been influenced by its current engagement in poor theory with its implied critique of theory weighed down by ornaments. Poor theory has echoes of *The Poverty of Theory*, the title of E. P. Thompson's 1978 polemic against Louis Althusser, the twentieth-century Marxist French philosopher, itself an echo of *Poverty of Philosophy*, Marx's nineteenth-century critique of yet another French thinker, the nineteenth-century Pierre-Joseph Proudhon. In the CTI project, *poor* is not used in the sense of appertaining to poverty, for even in a critical theory one does not want to give dignity to poverty by according it theory, but rather to accord dignity to the poor as they fight poverty, including, dare I say, poverty of theory. *Poor*, no matter the context of its use, implies the barest. Nothing could be barer than a grain of sand, and yet William Blake could talk of seeing the world in a grain of sand, eternity in an hour. Without the luxury of excess, the poor do the most with the least. Poor theory and its practice imply maximizing the possibilities inherent in the minimum.

Poor theory may also provide an antidote to the tendency of theory becoming like a kite that, having lost its mooring, remains floating in space with no possibility of returning to earth; or an even more needed critique of the tendency in the writing of theory to substitute density of words for that of thought, a kind of modern scholasticism. Instead of how many angels can stand on the head of a pin, we have how many words can stand on a line of thought. The terms in which E. P. Thompson once rejected Althusserism—or his interpretation of it at least—when he described it as "a sealed system in which concepts endlessly circulate, recognize and endlessly interrogate each other,"[3] would be even more apt as a description of aspects of modern literary scholarship, where "theory is forever collapsing into ulterior theory" and "in disallowing empirical enquiry, the mind is confined for ever within the compound of the mind."[4] Some presentations of theory have become like a gift carefully wrapped in layers of beautifully colored paper that the recipient, with great expectations, spends hours opening only to find a nondescript item inside. The recipient is supposed to appreciate the colorful thickness of the wrap. Of course, a gift of high quality, a diamond with a thousand rays of light, may also be wrapped up in layers of thick paper, and one may have to dig layers of dirt to reach a gem buried under the earth. Poor theory may simply remind us that density of words is not the same thing as complexity of thought; that such density, sometimes, can obscure clarity of thought. I like Taoism because the thought carried in the deceptively simple writing is anything but simple or static. I would like to think of poor theory as the Taoism of theory. Like Taoism, poor theory need not be static.

Even in social life, *poor* means being extremely creative and experimental in order to survive. The homeless try to make a home anywhere, even in places that do not suggest a home. A person without the wherewithal to buy clothes will pick pieces of cloth of whatever color, size, and shape and bring them together. He is clearly not worried about matching colors to please the eyes of an imagined critic at a cocktail party. Necessity drives him to yoke into one, a functional one, the different colors, shapes, and sizes. Then along comes a designer who may note the daring and the experimental in "this very interesting combination: maybe I can make a design out of that." A workman's clothes at a construction site will necessarily wear and tear. Soon, his pants become a network of threads, holes, and patches: then comes a designer, who may note the interesting pattern in "those weather-beaten trousers, those holes, that mismatch of colors." Soon a necessity at a construction site becomes an expensive luxury at college campuses and designer shops.

Some of the poor actually carry theory on their bodies. We have seen pictures of kids in ghettoes around the world wearing worn-out T-shirts or caps bearing the logos of various corporations: Nike, Coca-Cola, McDonalds, Mitsubishi, or Toyota, for instance. A logo in such a setting and context is no longer a commercial, advertising a product, but a pointer to a connection between the two extremes of ghetto poverty and corporate power. Some of the corporations are responsible for the sweatshop factories manned by children and women in free trade zones around the world. A friend told me of sighting a peasant in Mexico whose family had been driven from the land by large corporations: he was sporting a torn cap with the logo of John Deere, the company that made the big tractors that worked the land from which they had been driven. The man was neither advertising a product nor demonstrating against it, yet inadvertently he was making a connection.

The poor person's unintentional daring and experimentation comes from necessity. Necessity, after all, is the mother of invention. There are numerous inventions that have roots in having to do with the barest. Jazz was originally a poor person's version of an orchestra: unable to get all the instruments he saw in a regular ensemble, he did with the minimum he had and added sounds from whatever other materials he found around him. The Caribbean steel drum orchestra originates with the poor literally rescuing discarded oil drums and cutting them to different sizes to create the pans from which issue such unique, original sounds. The working poor of Trinidad and Tobago wrested beauty from the waste of the big oil corporations. Imagine making music from oil!

The great South African poet and sculptor Pitika Ntuli consciously works within that tradition of rescuing beauty from the wasted and discarded. His practice is inspired by the umbilical cord, the child's link to its mother. For humans, the environment is the mother. In South Africa, Pitika celebrated the umbilical cord's connection to the natural environment; the South African landscape permeated his every brush stroke in paintings and his every touch in sculpture. It was this connection, the claim of ownership, that the racist apartheid regime wanted to break when they drove him into exile. In the London of his exile, his new environment was not the lush bush and the natural colors of the African seasons, but metal, cobblestones, cement, glass, junk yards, and yes, racism. The racism, though not coded in laws, and the metallic urbanscape may have reminded him of South Africa and the urbanscape of Johannesburg and hence his loss, but still it was now his environment. Pitika could not just pass by a junkyard without finding objects for his art. His is poor theory of art in practice.

"Scrap yards, skips, derelict buildings, my rose gardens. I salvage weapons of war against ugliness. I attempt to humanize objects, exhaust pipes, gearboxes, saucepans; curses, insults, appreciation, grey clouds, monotonous terraces, odd patches of color in parks, human touch, frustration and hopes . . . my raw materials."[5]

He created a home out of exile. I was with him in London at the time, in the eighties, and when years later I visited him at his home in Kwazululand in a free South Africa,[6] I found his own yard full of the objects he had rescued from every junkyard and forest in South Africa. His practice was to create beauty out of the discarded, now in the united urban and rural landscape of his new South Africa. In parting, he gave me two quill-like shapes with tiny human heads at the tip. He had carved them out of elephant bones he had collected in the forest near his home in Kwazululand. They were no longer just bones. Storytellers, he told me. He knew I told stories. But he did not know that Njogu, Elephant, is my personal totem, the special name my mother gave me. An elephant who trumpets stories! Njogu also means the umbilical cord.

For me, coming from a background in performance, poor theory recalls not so much E. P. Thompson and Marx, but rather Grotowski when, in *Towards a Poor Theatre*, he proclaimed: "I propose poverty in theatre." No, not poverty as the end but as a means to riches. "The acceptance of poverty in theatre, stripped of all that is not essential to it revealed to us not only the backbone of the medium, but also the deep riches in the very nature of the art-form."[7] I come from a poor theater tradition, the traveling and community theater movements in East and Central Africa, not out of choice, not as something sought or arrived at, but as a starting point. Members of the Nairobi Free Traveling Theater, a product of the Literature Department of the University of Nairobi, performed pieces under all sorts of conditions, in all sorts of settings in the urban and rural areas of Kenya. Members of the Community Theater of Kamirithu Community Education and Cultural Center came from the villages, the factories, and the plantations in and around Limuru.[8] In both cases, they did not gradually learn to eliminate whatever was superfluous à la Grotowski, they started with the barest. They did not have to find that theater "can exist without make-up, without automatic costume and scenography, without lighting and sound effects," they started with the knowledge that they did not have them, they could not have them. A traveling theater cannot carry a stage and auditorium, it cannot have the luxury of choosing! It does with whatever is handed to it, making an aesthetic under circumstances not chosen by them. Their theatricality came from their bodies: for costumes, Kamirithu actors often used the same clothes they used for their daily lives. Yet their impact went beyond the campus and the village to the nation, and even beyond, spawning or joining similar streams in Africa.[9] The Nairobi Free Traveling Theater and, to a certain extent, the Kamirithu Theater, were byproducts of the Department of Literature that had replaced what hitherto had been known as the English Department.

Underlying these lectures is a story of how poor theory once produced a literature revolution at the University of Nairobi in the sixties and set in motion debates on postcolonial theory and literary studies that spread to the continent and beyond, to the world. I call it poor theory because initially it was no more than a few questions that simply demanded answers. The initial debates took place not in the academic corridors of the university, but in a rundown café on Koinange Street, Nairobi. In the process, the questions and the answers may have done more: produced a department that was organized entirely on the basis and vision of a world literature.

Although over the years there have always been talks of courses in world literature, this interest has intensified, recently seen, for instance, in the various efforts to organize courses in world literature; the publications of anthologies of world literature; and even theoretical debates on the concept in such works as *Debating World Literature*, edited by Christopher Prendergast, and *What Is World Liter-*

ature?, by David Damrosch, which contain stellar contributions by advocates of world literature. The latest is the MLA sponsored book, *Teaching of World Literature*, edited by David Damrosch, published in 2009.[10] Among the eminent contributors is Professor Jane Newman, writing on her experience of teaching a course on world literature at University of California, Irvine. So, UCI is right there in the mix. In light of the recent and current interest in the pedagogy, theory, and practice of world literature, it is worth revisiting the Nairobi debate as a contribution to further discussions on the theory and practice of world literature and the challenge it poses to the organization of literature in our times.

But the talks are less about the theory and practice of world literature than about the organization of the literary space and its impact on the politics of knowing, a continuation of my arguments about the politics of performance space and the enactments of power that I touched upon in my book *Penpoints, Gunpoints, and Dreams*. While each of the talks focuses on a fairly self-contained theme, the four talks are part of each other and they lead to the conclusions and challenges of the organization of literary global space posed in the third and fourth lectures. For literature, all the world is a stage.

The original lectures were delivered under the broad title "Hegelian Lord and Colonial Bondsman: Literature and the Politics of Knowing." They are informed by Hegelian dialectics in general, but, in particular, that of the master and the slave in *Phenomenology of the Spirit*. This is ironic for a person from Africa. In his lectures on the philosophy of history, this theorist of history as the march of freedom and reason in time and space made the most incredible claims about Africa as a land of childhood bypassed by that very history, and that, though slavery was inimical to freedom, it was somehow good for the African, presumably because it brought him from darkness into history, which Hegel saw as beginning in the East and finding its apotheosis in the West.[11] But the dialectic of the slave and the master has vast implications for the resolution of the unequal relationships of power underlying the totality of economics, politics, ethics, and aesthetics. Not surprisingly, the dialectic has intrigued many theorists of the psychology of the struggle for power, including Frantz Fanon,[12] who all realize that in the master and slave relationship, there is no neutrality in anything, even in the organization of any space, especially that of knowledge. A reorganization of a space, the same space, can, at the minimum, bring about different results and different perspectives, yielding, at the very least, different possibilities in literature, this wonderful product of what Tim Reiss, in his various works, calls fictive imagination.[13] In the end, literature is a collective contribution to the human.

The quality of contribution, whatever the quantity and diversity of sources, depends on how literature is read. James Baldwin talked of how he stopped hating Shakespeare the moment he was able to appropriate Shakespeare from the straitjackets of English imperial nationalism and place him in a more catholic space.[14] Like Baldwin, and, in the spirit of Wellek, I believe in the liberation of literature from the straightjackets of nationalism. Hence my use of the term *globalectics*.

Globalectics is derived from the shape of the globe. On its surface, there is no one center; any point is equally a center.[15] As for the internal center of the globe, all points on the surface are equidistant to it—like the spokes of a bicycle wheel that meet at the hub. Globalectics combines the global and the dialectical to describe a mutually affecting dialogue, or multi-logue, in the phenomena of nature and nurture in a global space that's rapidly transcending that of the artificially bounded, as nation and region. The global is that which humans in spaceships or on the international space station see: the dialectical is the internal dynamics that they do not see. Globalectics embraces wholeness, interconnectedness, equality of potentiality of parts, tension, and motion. It is a way of thinking and relating to the world, particularly in the era of globalism and globalization.

There is a personal angle to this: the debate about the organization of literature way back in the sixties set in motion a series of events and collisions that eventually led me not only to a maximum security prison and then exile, but also to my unrelenting interest in the aesthetics of decolonization and my current engagement in issues of linguistic Darwinism and feudalism. I hope these essays will show why a theory from a colony necessarily arises from and finds life in engagement.

I returned to Kenya from Leeds University, England, in 1967 and became a member of the English Department at the University of Nairobi. Within a year, I had joined two other colleagues not in the department, to write a document that called for its abolition.[1] The reaction was swift and intense. Meetings were held at all levels of the university: from the department to the faculty board of arts, the senate, and beyond the corridors of the university to the press and even the parliament. We had spoken the unspeakable, almost as if we had called for the end of the world. Over time, we were accused of many crimes. We wanted Shakespeare abolished and replaced by Caribbean, African-American, Asian, and Latin-American Marxists, including the most Marxist writers of all, V. S. Naipaul and Ralph Ellison. The debate and the consequences went beyond Nairobi to other universities in Africa and beyond, generating disputes, some of the earliest shots in what later became postcolonial theories. Why should the continued existence, or not, of an English department have generated so much fury and theory? I want to revisit the document, "On the Abolition of the English Department,"[2] by way of teasing out the ideological, epistemological, and pedagogical issues at the center of the dispute and their impact on my life and work in practice and theory.

Those who have read the recently released memoir of my childhood, *Dreams in a Time of War*, will know that I was born and came of age in a colony. My early childhood took place against the background of the Second World War. My education from elementary to college was in the period of the Mau Mau guerrilla war against the British settler state. My intellectual awakening was thus molded by colonialism and the anticolonial resistance that generated what the British prime minister, Harold Macmillan, famously described as a wind of change sweeping across the continent. I was a witness. When in 1959 I entered Makerere College, then affiliated with the University of London, East Africa was under colonial rule, with a state of emergency, all civil rights suspended, reigning over Kenya. Two years later we were celebrating Tanzanian independence; Uganda was next in 1962. Kenya's independence in 1963 coincided with my last semester at Makerere. I had entered Makerere as a colonial subject and emerged as a citizen of an independent country. It was not only in East Africa. The decade from the mid-'50s to the mid-'60s of the twentieth century saw country after country in Africa emerge from colonial status into nationhood. Overnight, colonial armies that had fought tooth and nail against nationalist demands became national armies. But no sooner were the new flags raised and the national anthems sung than there erupted army mutinies or attempted mutinies in Tanzania, Uganda, and Kenya. The wind of change had turned into a hurricane. The newly independent governments had to ask the former colonial overlords to bring in their armed forces to put down the rebellions. In the Congo, Belgium (its former colonizer), the United States, and the United Nations became embroiled in what ended with the brutal assassination of Patrice Lumumba and the assumption of power by a former colonel in the Belgian army, Mobutu Sese Seko. Chaos in the Congo, as the imbroglio was dubbed, became a metaphor for the cold war and its effect on the new states.

How could my study of four and half centuries of English literature, from Beowulf to Virginia Wolfe (or as Abiola Irele of Ibadan once described it—probably more mellifluously—from Spenser to Spender), speak to my colonial situation and the changes I was witnessing? My world was not reflected in any of those centuries into which the study of English had been periodized; it was certainly not the subject of the selected writers and literary texts. At least not directly. Heated discussions about D. H. Lawrence's *Lady Chatterley's Lover* and *Women in Love*, or the marriage intrigues of Jane Austen's middle class, interesting as they may have been in class, seemed far removed from the whirlwind. At times, those very discussions were seen as precisely part of what prevented self-awareness and the understanding of the whirlwind and the forces driving it. The famous poetic exchange between Molara Ogundipe of Nigeria and Felix Mnthali of Malawi best captures the ambivalence of the colonial student of English, with Jane Austen as the symbolic object of that ambivalence. In her poem, "To a 'Jane Austen class' at Ibadan University," Ogundipe calls upon them to ask why the Austen folk

carouse all day and do no work—play cards
at noon and dance the while—the while the land vanished
behind closures—mother's seeds into holds or marts—
and pliant life into pits—and in the south our souths, the
sorrow songs rake the skies—while death the autocrat
stalks both bond and free?[3]

Challenged, or as he says, stabbed, jabbed, and gored by her questions, Mnthali writes a response for Molara, "The Stranglehold of English Lit.," in which he wonders how her questions could have been asked and answered at Makerere, Ibadan, Dakar, or Fort Hare with Jane Austen's people at the center. With her "elegance of deceit," Jane Austen had lulled "the sons and daughters of the dispossessed into a calf-love with irony and satire around imaginary people" while history went on mocking "the victims of branding irons and sugar plantations that made Jane Austen's people wealthy beyond repair." Then comes the declaration:

Eng. Lit., my sister,
Was more than a cruel joke—
it was the heart
of alien conquest.[4]

It might have tempered Mnthali's and Ogundipe's reactions to the discipline if some of these writers had been read through a view from the colony: that is, in the context of some of the far-reaching movements of their time—slavery and colonialism, for instance—so that instead of just praising James Boswell as this great biographer of Samuel Johnson, it might also have been pointed out that Boswell was a defender of slavery; or, to balance that, point out that Samuel Coleridge pamphleteered for the abolition of slavery, and his albatross in "The Rime of the Ancient Mariner" could have been a reference to what he would have seen as the moral burden of slavery hanging on the psyche of the trading nations. And would they not have embraced William Wordsworth in his sonnet to Toussaint L'Overture, the liberator of Haiti, languishing in Napoleon's dungeon! For Wordsworth, in this sonnet at least, Toussaint, though alone in deep dungeon's den, was still the embodiment of "man's unconquerable mind." Thus, depending on the eyes through which they were read, the texts would occasionally yield direct or elusive glimpses of possible connections, as through a broken mirror as when King Lear in the storm rails against unequal justice between the poor and the rich or when Caliban protests the loss of his labor and the land to Prospero in Shakespeare. Ogundipe and Mnthali, both outstanding students of English, were reading the literature through a view from the colony and were asking questions that would not have come up in the official classroom. Caribbean literary thinkers, principally the Barbadian George Lamming in the early sixties, the Martiquan Aimé Césaire in the late sixties, and the Cuban Retamar in the early seventies were revisiting English literature, reclaiming and appropriating Caliban as a figure of antiresistance. Thus, a consistent view from the colony would have made, in our situation, a revolutionary reading and reception of the texts, snatching them from the jaws of alien conquest. In the world today, some of the most penetrating readings of the same texts have come from theorists from the colony: Gayatri Spivak, Edward Said, Peter Nazareth, Homi Bhaba, Simon Gikandi, Abiola Irele, and Anthony Appiah, and, from Irvine, Ketu Katrak and R. Radhakrishnan, to mention but a few. Clearly, the view from the colony was not dominant in the classrooms of our times.

The criticism that went with the texts did not provide an adequate framework that made coherent sense of the elusive glimpses, where we could see comparative connections or disconnections with our situation. Literary criticism and theory of the time paid attention to close readings. Within a wider theoretical framework, close reading can turn every text into a treasure house. It is the one approach that can prevent theory from becoming the kite that has lost its moorings or prevent critics from becoming attorneys and judges who argue their cases, in prosecution, defense, or judgment, without adducing reasons from the evidence. It can be an antidote to the tendency, probably derived from Plato's notion of divine madness and possession in poets, to treat writers as mindless geniuses and use their work as simply a platform to launch a critic's flight to space. Close reading should be an important companion to poor theory. But without that broad political-cum-ideological framework, close reading and obsession with formalistic elements can turn into attempts to squeeze the world of the literary text through the eye of the critical needle, a contribution to poverty of theory. It's like entering a treasure trove and counting the items inside without an awareness of their value, unable to relate them to anything outside.

Within the classroom, among the dominant critical texts were T. S. Eliot's "Tradition and the Individual Talent," Matthew Arnold's *Culture and Anarchy*, and F. R. Leavis's *The Great Tradition*. Arnold's tirades against the intellectual torpor (or torpitude) of the aristocracy and the philistinism of the middle classes produced more heat than light; the social conditions he berated were abstract. I mean that we could only imagine his aristocracy and middle classes. T. S. Eliot's tradition, the prose extension of the mutual containment of times present, past, and future of his "Burnt Norton," was European through and through. His essay could be seen as providing the reason he, an American, reinvented himself as an Englishman, even converting to the High Anglican Church. America, with its heterogeneous roots in indigenous America, Africa, and Europe, could not have offered him the kind of historical sense evidenced in the European tradition from Homer to the present. His objective correlatives were to be found (scattered) in the European cultural temporal landscape rather than America. It could be argued that he did look beyond Europe to Eastern religions and philosophies evidenced by his many allusions, to the Bhagavad Gita in particular, but it was the European tradition, the Anglo-Catholic, that provided the historical pole around which these could cohere. F. R. Leavis's insistence on the moral significance of literature (his arbitrary choice of writers and texts to make the Great Tradition) was fascinating, but it was difficult to track down that significance beyond the ethical and aesthetic boundaries of the texts of the members of his Great Tradition. The most coherent were not these critical minds of English literature but those from the Greek academy of Aristotle and Plato. Aristotle's *Poetics* and Plato's *Republic* were some of the foundational theoretical texts of our studies. But even here, the extraction of the formalistic elements fitted into that overall critical approach.

The result of the close reading of texts (which I value to this day) and the formalistic could be seen in our undergraduate essays, mine in particular, in which the main focus was on how the narrative was put together, from sentences and paragraphs to the structure and the overall balance of moral forces in the text. The weight of Leavis lay heavily on my papers, mostly those on Joseph Conrad. In terms of evaluation of the literary text, these critical voices, particularly Eliot's, no doubt, left a mark on our vocabulary, particularly the notion of a writer having to hear all the voices that had gone before him. But the gulf between the text without context and the colonial world, to use the Edward Saidian terms of reference, remained wide and deep. From the English classroom, there were no critical bridges to help us cross the gulf so that we could make sense of the howling winds outside the walls of our Makerere ivory tower: hence Molara Ogundipe's questions and Felix Mnthali's response.

The bridges came from outside the formal English classroom, from African and Caribbean fiction. This fiction, even though in English, would not have fitted into Eliot's depth of tradition and history for it was a twentieth-century phenomenon. There were two major waves: the first took place before the 1950s, with the examples of C. R. L. James, Claude Mackay, and Alfred Mendes in the Caribbean and S. E. K. Mqhayi, B. Wallet Vilakazi, and the brothers H. I. E. and R. R. R. Dhlomo in South Africa. The second wave consisted of the postwar emigrations of Caribbean workers and intellectuals, a movement dramatized in George Lamming's novel, *The Emigrants*. This was a kind of Caribbean literary renaissance that gave to the world such luminaries as V. S. Naipaul, George Lamming, Andrew Salkey, and Samuel Selvon. It is the work of this wave that reached us, in bits and pieces, at Makerere, mostly through hearsay, the library, and private hands. In the works of Peter Abrahams from South Africa, Chinua Achebe from Nigeria, and George Lamming from Barbados, to take only a few examples, were characters and relationships clearly reflective of the howling winds. It was amazing to find that a novel could capture the drama of the colonial and the anticolonial while obeying all the aesthetic laws of fiction. It spoke directly to my experience. It was fiction that first gave us a theory of the colonial situation.

Fiction as theory? Can we in fact think of fiction, the novel, as writing theory? We have to go back to the original meaning of theory in Greek, *theoria*, meaning a view and a contemplation. View assumes a viewer, a ground on which to stand, and what is viewed from that standpoint. A view is also a framework for organizing what is seen and a thinking about the viewed. Fiction is the original poor theory. Confronted with an environment that they could not always understand, the human invented stories to explain it. The understanding of nature begins with its personification. The very origins of the universe are explained in myths and stories. Egyptian, Yoruba, Greek, Chinese, and Indian mythologies explain the multifaceted forces of nature by giving them dynamic personalities derived from the way they manifest themselves to the human. Classical orature of all societies have stories of the why, how, when, and what of the phenomenon of nature: how the leopard got its spots, how the dog came to live with humans, why people die, etcetera. All these are different views of the universe and for many years they were taken by the cultures that produced them as real explanations of natural and supernatural phenomena. The Indian epics, the Mahabharata in particular, offer a theory of the physical and moral universe out of which comes the sacred Hindu text, the Bhagavad Gita, a kind of sermon from the battlefield. In the Homeric poems *The Odyssey* and *The Iliad*, humans and the gods interact even in the conduct of human affairs. The two were basic texts of the education of youth in terms of the desirable ideals of *Arete* (excellence), *Dike* (justice), *Aidos* (duty), and *Kleos* (glory).

Plato, reacting to the mythological as a theory of nature and society, disparaged poetry—poets are liars, three times removed from reality, after the realms of ideas or forms and the material world—in favor of reason. He wrote *The Republic*, a theory of an ideal state based on reason, in opposition to the Homeric state, based on myths. In him the mythological consciousness of the Homeric imagination was replaced by a rational consciousness. But even in *The Republic*, Plato utilized myths and parables. For instance, he used the allegory of the cave to explain his theory of forms, and the myth of Er to explain, among other things, the cosmos and afterlife. Both Sigmund Freud and Carl Gustav Jung see myths as guides into the psychic universe: in the case of Freud, his theory of the Oedipus complex was the nucleus of all neuroses, while Jung rewrote Platonic ideal forms in terms of the archetypes he found in myths.

Myths, stories, and parables are all products of what Reiss calls the fictive imagination. The novel, like the myth and the parable, gives a view of society from its contemplation of social life, reflecting it, mirror-like, but also reflecting upon it, simultaneously. The novelistic is akin to the scientific outlook in method. The scientist collects data in the lab or in the field. He observes it, tries out different combinations, and comes up with a theory. The scientist may begin with a hypothesis, but that hypothesis may be modified by the logic of the data at hand. Novelists draw from the data of life that they have noted with their senses of touch, sight, hearing, and smell. They see patterns and connections that their mind helps coalesce into something that transcends the individual particular objects of their senses into a kind of universality in which readers of different ages, climes, and gender can see themselves and the world in which they live, differently. Like the scientist, they may begin with a hypothesis or an image, but this is modified or altered altogether by the logic of the plot. In his *Dialogic Imagination,* Bakhtin talks about the dialogic character of the novel, meaning the multiplicity of voices. But the dialectical is probably a better characterization of its multifaceted temporal and spatial reach. The novel mimics, contemplates, clarifies, and unifies many elements of reality in terms of quality and quantity. It helps organize and make sense of the chaos of history, social experience, and personal inner lives. As a creative process, it mimics the creation of the universe as order from chaos.

Let me illustrate with my own beginnings as a writer. I am on record, in several interviews, as saying that my writing was an attempt to understand myself and history, to make sense of the apparently irrational forces of the colonial and postcolonial.[5] My experience of Kenya had been as a white settler colony into which I was born. Everything had been in terms of black and white. White was wealth and power. Black was poverty and subjection to another. But certain happenings, even in colonial Kenya, were beginning to challenge that neat demarcation and I had no vocabulary by which to understand and name what I was seeing and feeling. I turned to the journalistic essay. As an undergraduate at Makerere, completely outside the classroom, I started contributing articles to the Kenyan press, about fifty between 1961 and 1964, mostly under my own column "As I See It" in the *Sunday Nation*. But despite the quantity and variety of issues tackled, I never felt that my literary journalism had made me come to grips with the whirlwind any more than I had through the class essay. How could an article really capture the complexity of what I had experienced in colonial Kenya? The blood in the streets; the dead guerrillas hung on trees as a public spectacle; the horror stories of white officers collecting ears, noses, eyes, genitalia, or even heads of the vanquished as trophies! The tortures in the internment camps and concentration villages were symbolized by the horror at Hola where in 1959 eleven political internees were tortured to death in a couple of days. Fortunately, news of it somehow came out and reached the world. There were many horrors whose knowledge never went beyond the location of their commission. There was also the violence of the guerrilla army not always directed at the guilty party. Horror multiplied was still horror.

One event in particular stood out. It was the day, in 1955, that I returned to my village after my first semester at a boarding school. I was looking forward to my reunion with my family, my mother especially; I could even picture her smile. Communication in those days, beyond word of mouth, did not really exist for rural folk. On arrival, I was met by the sight of ashes and burnt debris. Not only our house! The entire village had been razed to the ground by the British forces and the entire community relocated into a concentration village.[6] Years later when I read Césaire's description of the havoc wrought by colonialism in terms of "societies drained of their essence, cultures trampled underfoot, institutions undermined, lands confiscated, religions smashed, magnificent artistic creations destroyed, extraordinary possibilities wiped out,"[7] I would think of this scene of deracination of everything that had been part of my identity within a particular period and place, but mostly recall the sheer incomprehension and the reversal of my expectations. These haunted me. The prose essay could not quite order the chaos of that experience.

I turned to fiction to help me understand the encounter with chaos. My short story, *The Return*, which I published in 1961 in *Transition Magazine*, was about a Mau Mau guerrilla fighter who returns home after years in a British concentration camp, hoping to reconnect with life as he had left it. He imagines a new beginning rooted in the family life he had left behind. The reality is a shock. And only the sight of a river, with water endlessly flowing and yet remaining the same river, makes him come to terms with change. I did not know that Heraclitus had made the same point in ancient Greece. The action is dominated by the returnee; its duration—the beginning, the middle, and the denouement—unfolds in one day, and, although we follow him on the road, the focus is on the home to which he is coming back. I had stuck to the Aristotelian unities of time and place and character, a case of borrowing form from another time and place and context and filling it with a lived content from another place and time. It was also an instance of what had been discussed in the classroom intruding into my world.

This story, anthologized to this day, had a more universal reach than any of my fifty articles, which are hardly ever cited, except as footnotes in references to the literary journalism of my youth. The reversal of expectations, the clash between expectations and reality, helped me clarify the conception of tragedy, from Sophocles to Chinua Achebe. What Aristotle said of poetry, that it was finer and more philosophical than history since poetry expresses the universal and history only the particular, is probably truer of the novel. The novel analyzes, synthesizes, has a view, and reaches out to beyond the space and time of its location. If science is a theory of material nature, and literature in general, Reiss's fictive imagination, a science of nurture, fiction, in particular, can be seen as a theory of felt experience. It was to the novel that I turned for a way of ordering my history. My first three novels—*The River Between, Weep Not Child,* and *A Grain of Wheat*—were set in the different phases of Kenyan history from the colonial to the immediate postcolonial period—independence and after. Through them, I came to realize that I most seem to understand the inner logic of social processes when I am deep inside imaginative territory. Writing *Wizard of the Crow,* for instance, helped me better understand the forces underlying both globalization and globalism than my more conscious analyses of the same phenomena.

But the novel, though itself a view of society, cannot talk about itself or its relationship to others. It cannot contemplate itself, despite attempts at metafiction like *The Life and Opinions of Tristram Shandy* by Laurence Sterne or the *nouveau roman* of Robert Grille. For in the end, the novel, whatever its form, has to deal with lived experience. Fiction as theory had its limitations, for it could not deal with itself; it could not read other fiction. It needed lenses with which to view it as a whole and its relationship to society and history. So despite my fiction and journalism, I still did not have an adequate conception and comprehensive view of the colonial process and the immediate postindependence era. My intellectual life was still centered on English literature. I still had to find a way of reading English literature and the new literature to make them yield more about my world. But where was I to turn for this?

In Leeds, while researching Caribbean literature, I came into contact with Marxian dialects. Marxian dialects were of course essentially Hegelian dialects, but rooted in history and actual social being. Marx was to Hegel what Aristotle was to Plato. One moved from the material to the ideal rather than from the ideal to the material. But in Marx, the ideal could also affect the material, a mutual effect captured in his statement that "theory also becomes a material force as soon as it has gripped the masses."[8] Mind and body were not separate spheres of the human. They were interwoven. Change was a constant theme in nature, history, and human thought, but it was not mechanical or linear. Marx's metaphors could light up connections in the most apparent contradictions, as when he talked of capitalism coming into history dripping with blood or when he compared bourgeois progress to the pagan idol who drank nectar, but only from the skulls of the slain. Motion involved contraries. Marx made me reflect on many things including my conception of history and narrative practice. I started, in a conscious way, to seek connections in phenomena even in the seemingly unconnected. He challenged the linear development of history, the formative principle of my first two novels, *The River Between* and *Weep Not Child*. Marx, aided no doubt by my teachers— for instance Arnold Kettle, the author of the voluminous *Introduction to the English Novel*—changed my approaches to reading texts. One could separate the chaff and the grain in the same work. Interest in Marx also led us to other thinkers, Jean-Paul Sartre, for instance, whose questions and ideas about commitment in literature intensified our own concern with what English literature had to say about our colonial situation.

After Marx released me from a one-dimensional view of reality, I could now go back to texts I had already read and find a whole world I had not seen earlier. In the London working-class poor of Dickens's world I found echoes of the colonial world, making it easier for me later to understand Césaire when he talked of the European bourgeoisie as having simultaneously created the problem of the colonial subject abroad and that of the working class at home. The poor at home and the colonial subject were products of the same process; in that sense Dickens's sarcastic jibe at telescopic philanthropy in *Bleak House* made a lot of sense, as did his hinting at the bourgeois gentleman as a product of colonial labor in *Great Expectations*.

Even Conrad could yield more than a struggle and balance of moral forces. He located his major works in the heartlands of imperialism. Images of quest and acquisition of rubber, gold, or copper in Africa, the Far East, or in South America dominate the action. In *Heart of Darkness*, he talks of colonial conquests of the earth as "taking it away from those who have a different complexion or slightly flatter noses than ourselves."[9] He dramatizes the corruption of the erstwhile phi-

lanthropist cum carrier of enlightenment Kurtz, who ends up deco-
rating the walls of his colonial palatial grounds with human skulls,
reminiscent of Marx's image of the pagan idol who drank nectar only
from the skulls of the slain. *Nostromo*, which I had earlier analyzed in
terms of an interplay of moral forces of trust, betrayal, and marriage
to material interests as opposed to moral ideals, now opened itself
in terms of the struggle between labor and capital (a novel that years
later, as a visiting professor of English and comparative literature at
Yale, I would teach side by side with Lenin's "Imperialism, the High-
est Stage of Capitalism"). The merger of bank and industry to make
financial capital that the Marxist Lenin talked about in boring figures
and statistics had been dramatized in *Nostromo* by the non-Marxist
Anglophile Joseph Conrad. Moral issues and choices were there but
they did not exist in an ethereal realm. Ironically, as I point out in
my memoirs, it was in Shakespeare, the imperial literary export, the
icon of the genius of British imperial culture, where these echoes were
mostly pronounced. His texts were full of bloody struggles for power.
In the Kenyan streets, Macbeth's bloody dagger was a historical reality and no longer a figment of imagination. No text shows better the
exploitation of race and color prejudice than *Othello* in the manipula-
tive hands of Iago. The case of the New Orleans magistrate who, in
twenty-first-century America, would not marry white with black was
a figure from *Othello*. *The Merchant of Venice* in the character of Shy-
lock expresses the pain of being the object of racist reductionism and
stereotype. In their dialectical view of reality, Hegel and Marx could
have been expanding on William Blake when he talked of seeing the
world in a grain of sand, eternity in an hour.[10] Or when he said that
without contraries there was no progression, that attraction and re-
pulsion were necessary for human progress.[11] All in all, the dialectical
view of the literary text had opened my eyes to the infinite beauty and
complexity of the English text.

But while the issues of race, color, and colonialism could be in-
ferred through dialectical lenses from a closer reading of the texts,
they remained what they had been: glimpses of the colony from the
imperial center. Marxian Literary theorists, like Lukács, were equally
inadequate for comprehending issues of race and color. His studies in

European realism or history and class consciousness were stripped of their colonial side. C. L. R. James, the celebrated writer of *The Black Jacobins*, had noted this lacuna in such European studies and declared that while the race question was subsidiary to the class question in politics, "to think of imperialism in terms of race is disastrous . . . to neglect the racial factor as merely incidental is an error only less grave than to make it fundamental."[12] It was probably similar reasoning that made Césaire, accused of racism for bringing the black dimension to class issues, declare: Marx is all right, but we need to complete Marx.[13]

The negritude movement of Aimé Césaire, Léopold Sédar Senghor, and Léon Damas was an attempt to complete Marx. A cultural reflection of Pan-Africanism, or blackism on a world scale, it was literary practice and a theory of race sometimes using race and class interchangeably. Césaire defined negritude as a concrete rather than abstract coming into consciousness.[14] Sartre's description of it as antiracist racism, the negative phase of the Hegelian triad that would itself be negated to yield a mediated nonracialism, captured its major themes of black humanism. Senghor's poem "To New York," with its tribute to the Harlem Renaissance, is structured on this Hegelian triad as applied to race matters. The persona in the poem on his first visit to New York is probably Senghor himself, who visited the city for the first time in 1950. The (unmediated) thesis is Western civilization, symbolized by Manhattan, whose impressive façade of skyscrapers and bridges across the Hudson are transformed in his consciousness to one of blue metallic eyes, muscles of steel and stone skins, the city of Hygienic love and environmental disaster, drained of humanity; the negating phase is Harlem of black blood and dancing feet, the Harlem of the Harlem Renaissance; the synthesis, New York, once the black blood is allowed into it, the blood cleansing the rust from the steel joints like an oil of life. Even Césaire's long poem, *Return to My Native Land*, with its critique of a Western industrial civilization emptied of humanism and its hoorays for those who never invented or discovered anything, but whose humanism is captured in the image of delving deep in the red flesh of soil, ends with possibilities for a synthesis, a reconciliation, for it was not true that the work of man was finished and "no race holds a monopoly of beauty, of intelligence, of strength and there is room for all at the rendez-vous of conquest" of the human.[15] But though Negritude was elevating as poetry and imagery, its theoretical articulation could be mystical in its metaphysical abstraction, as when Senghor tried to explain the difference between black Africa and the West in the mellifluous metaphysical nonsense of his statement "Emotion is Negro as Reason is Greek."

In its theoretical formulation, despite Césaire's definition of it as a coming into concrete consciousness, negritude as theory seemed far from explaining the thisness and materiality of the colonial whirlwind. Its Anglophone critics took issue with what they saw as its abstraction of Being from concrete being. Among the critics was the late Esk'ia Mphahlele who seized on this lack of focus on the concreteness of reality. Wole Soyinka mocked its rhetoric by saying that a tiger did not sing about its tigritude, it pounced, thus expressing its being with concrete action. At times the critique confused negritude as a theory with its practice because some of the poetry is of infinite beauty and power and captured the anguish of the black colonial condition. There is really nothing abstract about Césaire's poetry or in the fighting poetry of Léon Damas, two of the three founding musketeers of the Negritude movement. Whatever its limitation as practice, method, and theory, negritude had the effect of opening eyes to a vast black literature that embraced Africa, Black America, and Latin America and was something we could only encounter outside the formal English classroom at home or abroad.

And then came Frantz Fanon. Fanon was born in Martinique, a French colony, and educated in Paris. He later relocated to Algeria, where he initially worked for the French administration, before abandoning it to work for the Algerian resistance against French settler occupation. He was thus born in a colonial situation and died while still in the service of a struggle to end colonialism. His book *The Wretched of the Earth* made a big impact on the minds of the students who had come to Leeds from the colonies and former colonies.[16] Fanon had published other books, the best known of which was *Black Skin, White Masks*, but they did not have the same impact.

Fanonism was a combination of psychoanalysis and Marxian-cum-Hegelian dialects applied to the colonial situation from inside the colony by a student of philosophy, a practicing psychiatrist, and an active revolutionary. Where in *Black Skin, White Masks* Fanon had used the combination, particularly the dialectic of master and slave, to analyze white and black largely as metaphysical and psychological entities, in *The Wretched of the Earth* the combination is turned on the concrete material situation. Hegel's master and slave dialectic occurs in the chapter of the *Phenomenology* on self-consciousness in which he powerfully shows that self-consciousness is attained only as a result of a struggle for recognition between two consciousnesses. In *Black Skin, White Masks*, the master and bondsman of the Hegelian dialect become white and black, and the terrain of their struggle is largely Antillean; in *The Wretched of the Earth*, they become the colonizer and the colonized and the context is worldwide.

It is in *The Wretched of the Earth* that Fanon brought out the real, historical violence at the heart of the *bildung*, a formative education of the spirit,[17] of Hegel's *Phenomenology of Spirit*. The incredible opening chapter concerning violence is the Hegelian "trial by death," "the life and death struggle" for the subjugation of the hitherto free by the equally hitherto free, but now in a real concrete situation of the colonizer and colonized. Just as the master and slave in the Hegelian dialectic know one another, the settler and the native know each other, for both pairs are mirror images of each other, with a difference: in the dialectic, the he-who-would-be master faces another, an identical he-who-would-be master. In Fanon, the colonial master and colonized bondsman see their dialectical opposites. But where in Hegel the struggle to death takes place between two initially independent entities resulting in master and slave, in *The Wretched of the Earth* the same takes place after the colonizer is already the master of the colonized. In both cases, violence is a *bildung*, a formative education. In Hegel it forces one of the two consciousnesses to recognize his adversary as the Master; in Fanon, it forces the active colonizer to recognize the independence of his menial adversary. In Hegel violence is formative of master and slave. In Fanon, it is a formative of the independence of the subjugated and, hopefully, the end of the conditions that create the duo. In Hegel the violence is for subjugation, but the result is a new spiritual formation of the subjected in his awareness of his independence; in Fanon, it is for liberation. In both, violence is the midwife of history, "of every old society pregnant with a new one."[18]

It is thus absurd to call Fanon the apostle of violence, as *Newsweek* once described him, anymore than Hegel. But one can see the basis for the label. The economic, political, and cultural corpses, consequences of colonial and anticolonial struggles, were strewn all over the pages of *The Wretched of the Earth*, but they merely reflected and made theoretical sense of the violence in all the settler states of Kenya, South Africa, Algeria, Zimbabwe, and beyond Africa. For Fanon both colonialism and decolonization were violent processes and the results as he shows in the chapter on colonial wars and mental disorder were not a pretty thing for individual minds in either side of the struggle.

In the theory of global colonialism and decolonization, *The Wretched of the Earth* once again linked Africa to Asia and Latin America. The questions it raised were reflected in much of the literature from Africa and the former colonial world as a whole. One of the most important questions posed vis-à-vis the colonized was one of identity: "Because it is a systematic negation of the other person and a furious determination to deny the other person all attributes of humanity, colonialism forces the people it dominates to ask themselves the question constantly: 'in reality who am I?'"[19]

For me, this theoretical mix of fiction, Marx, Fanon, and new literatures was a far cry from the days of combing through the pages of Samuel Johnson via his biographer, James Boswell, or those of Samuel Coleridge, Matthew Arnold, T.S. Eliot, and F. R. Leavis or leafing through the pages of studies in philology to make a sense of where and how I fit in English national literature as a colonial child.

It was with this mix, an awareness of the vast literatures in Africa, Asia, and Latin America and the questions of identity bubbling in my mind, that I returned to Kenya in 1967, but, to quote from T. S. Eliot's *Second Coming*, no longer at ease with the postindependence moment. The unease was reflected in my third novel, *A Grain of Wheat*, but explicitly in the preface where I said that although the characters were fictional, the situation and the problems depicted in the novel were real, "sometimes too painfully real for the peasants who fought the British yet who now see all that they fought for being put on one side."[20] The unease deepened when, on joining the English Department, I was confronted by the still intact specter of Spenser to Spender, except for a course on African literature that Esk'ia Mphahlele had taught the year before, but with his departure for Zambia, was taught no more. The four and half centuries of English national literature were still at the center of literary education. Nothing had changed. It was reminiscent of the clerk in charge of one of the trading stations in Conrad's *Heart of Darkness*, so mindful of his appearance and dress, starched collar and all, as if protecting them from the surrounding turmoil.

Where was the place of the vast literature that I had now become aware of? In a discussion paper presented by the acting chair of English about the changes the department might make to reflect postcolonial developments, it was clearly stated that the principle was still the need for a study of the historic continuity of a single culture, English of course, with other streams admitted in time. One can hear echoes of T. S. Eliot, tradition and individual talent, in the phrase continuity of a single culture. English was the great tradition with African as an ancillary to be admitted into the master narrative as time and space allowed. In our counter-paper, we shot back rhetorically: if there is need for the study of the historical continuity of a single culture, why can't this be African? It was not deliberate, but the title, "On the Abolition of the English Department," had clear echoes of the abolition of slavery. The paper, though, was not a call for the abolition of English literature. In asking for a change of name from the English Department to simply Literature and the reorganization of the curriculum so that African literature and related literature would constitute the inner circle with English and other European literatures in translation in the outer circles, it simply questioned the cognitive process, what was central and what was ancillary and their relationship in the acquisition of knowledge in a postcolonial context. It questioned the role of the organization of knowledge in the production of the colonial and postcolonial subject. I shall deal with this and the education of the colonial bondsman in the next chapter.

THE EDUCATION OF
THE COLONIAL BONDSMAN

2 The celebrated pairing of master and bondsman in Hegel's dialectic makes it clear that the two adversaries are initially independent beings before the conquest of one by the other. Each is equally an independent in-itself and for-itself. Their postconquest being is the unequal relationship of the master—the independent consciousness whose essential nature is to be for itself—and the bondsman—the dependent consciousness whose essential nature is simply to live or be for another.[1] But though their postconquest relationship is one of victor and vanquished, it is de facto one of parasite and producer. A parasite grows, feeds, and shelters in a different organism, the host. It gets everything from the host and gives it nothing. Hence, a dialectically changed reality emerges: it is the master who is dependent where the bondsman, by making and identifying or seeing himself in what he produces, is independent. Where the producer can do without the parasite, the parasite cannot do without the producer. But how come the de facto dependent is still the master of the de facto independent, for where the latter proposes the former disposes? The dialect seems silent on this, or rather the bondsman would seem to be content with simply finding himself in service and work.[2] It is as if the self-consciousness of his independence through his self-identification with the independent being of the things he makes gives him merely psychological satisfaction. Hegel does not pursue the political question: whether or not self-conscious independence will become political liberation. The reasons for this seeming contradiction, continued independence in bondage and continued dependence in lordship, are implicit in Hegel's very concepts of (being) in itself and for itself, concepts later elaborated in *The Science of Logic*. The lord is a consciousness (being) in itself and for itself: the bondsman is an existent in itself but for another.

We have to be cautious in drawing conclusions, for the dialectic is only a small section of a larger argument. But it is a self-contained parable that, like Plato's allegory of the cave, tempts us to raise questions about what it does or does not do. Although one can go beyond the dialectic and assume that the bondsman, out of his self-consciousness, will go on to fight for his liberty, this logical next step may not always follow. The coercive element of physical force may bend the body, but an even more coercive element of mental force may compel a distorted consciousness of the reality of their actual relationship. The fact is, the master is in control of both coercive forces: the physical and the mental. He has the monopoly of education, the content, the form, the space, and the order of its delivery. Were the mental coercion to succeed, the bondsman would even come to express gratitude for the spiritual benefits he has garnered from the master. Hegel's trial by death would seem to be silent on the mental coercion; or rather, it is only implicit in the sense that their struggle to death must include all the resources at their disposal.

Hegel's dialectic of master and slave, or lord and bondsman, needs supplementing by two other literary pairings: Prospero and Caliban in Shakespeare's *The Tempest* and Crusoe and Friday in Defoe's *Robinson Crusoe*. When Prospero and Caliban first meet, they correspond to Hegel's two independent consciousnesses. They are both emigrants to the island, although Caliban is native born. They have their own independent pasts and knowledge. Prospero has book knowledge. Caliban has all the knowledge of the island's history and geography. In fact, Caliban has a personal relationship with the island. He finds it full of sounds and sweet airs that give him delight.

> Sometimes a thousand twangling instruments
> Will hum about mine ears, and sometime voices
> That, if I then had waked after long sleep,

Will make me sleep again: and then, in dreaming,
The clouds methought would open and show riches
Ready to drop upon me that, when I waked,
I cried to dream again. (act 3, scene 2)

Their initial exchange was of two apparent equals. In exchange for water with berries, strokes, flattery, and knowledge of the stars, Caliban loved him

And show'd thee all the qualities o' the isle
The fresh springs, brine-pits, barren place and fertile. (act 1, scene 2)

The text does not tell us how Prospero, the possessor of book magic, came to subjugate Caliban, and whether or not they went through the phase of what Hegel calls, "trial by death" or "a life-and-death struggle," but we can assume that they did. The violence is suggested by the rock to which Caliban is chained or the threats of torture hurled at Ariel for begging for liberty in exchange for his loyalty and meekness. The result fits into the post-violence second phase of the Hegelian paradigm. Caliban is the producer, Prospero the parasite. Prospero admits his dependence.

We cannot miss him: he does make our fire,
Fetch in our wood and serves in offices
That profit us. (act 1, scene 2)

But knowledge and education play a role. It is worth noting again that when they first meet, it's Caliban who has the knowledge of the island, its history, and ecology. He passes that knowledge to Prospero. It's not the way Prospero sees their encounter. When they first met, he now tells Caliban, you did not know yourself, your language was mere babble. I gave you purpose. Caliban curses Prospero in the very language with which Prospero had hoped to tame him. He rebels, in words at least, but it does not alter the fact that the structure and organization of knowledge inevitably reinforces the master and servant relationship.

The "I gave you knowledge" of Prospero is repeated in the great education scene in Defoe's *Robinson Crusoe* where Crusoe names the man Friday, marking the day that he discovers him. The identity of Friday thus begins with the day that Crusoe discovers him. Crusoe introduces himself as master. Although Friday and Crusoe have not fought each other to death à la Hegel's master and bondsman, their relationship is that of the slave, Friday, who produces, and the master, Crusoe, who disposes. Crusoe's power comes from his possession of a gun, an instrument of violence, but also his organization and delivery of education. The order of knowledge defines and reinforces the terms of their relationship. Crusoe is the teacher; Friday has nothing to teach. Even were Crusoe and Friday to read the same texts, these would still come as a gift from the master. Of course Friday may put the knowledge from the book to different ends, like his literary predecessor, Caliban, who curses in the language of the master, but once again, as in the case of Caliban, this would not alter the facts and the intended results of a Crusoe-controlled structure and organization of knowledge: the definition of reality from the master's perspective.

The use of knowledge to obscure reality and force a certain perception of reality as the norm is not a matter of parables in philosophy, theater, and fiction. During the era of slave trade and plantation slavery, there were tons of publications that rationalized it as the norm, so much so that later, in the American Declaration of Independence, the word *people* clearly did not include African Americans, indigenous peoples, or women. The slave could do without the plantation owner, but the plantation owner could never do without the slave. Without the slave there is no plantation; but without the owner, there would still be land, on which work can produce things for the worker's own use. In today's world, labor can do without capital; but capital can never do without labor. If capital went on strike, people would still work on the land or on machines in factories, make things for use, even exchange, but if labor went on strike, it would end the life of capital—its dominance, at least. Yet our habit is to view labor as dependent on capital, and, in today's world, given the dominance of capital, especially in its mutation as financial capital, that habitual view may seem obvious and given. The Agricultural South has all the natural resources the Industrial North needs, but the South is perceived and perceives itself as the dependent. Within each country, industry is master to the more fundamental agriculture. In capitalism, the finance part has come to be the master of the industrial, which Marx described as the case of the dead ruling over the living. A press on the keyboard of a computer or a Blackberry, or an order spoken into a cell phone, can move money from one country to another in seconds, bringing to a sudden stop buildings and whole industries. The reign of the dead (debts, credit cards, borrowing from the future, etc.) over the living has come to be accepted, through numerous impressions on the mind, as natural, an inevitable normality, the engine of modern society and dynamic mover of globalization.

It is clear that in the paradigm of master and slave, the master will have a view of philosophy, religion, history, human nature, education, and organization of knowledge that conflicts fundamentally with that of the adversarial opposite. In his or her concept of history, the master, like Prospero, will emphasize that there reigned ignorance before his arrival, or that there had always been masters and bondsmen. In philosophy, the master will emphasize the unchanging character of human nature, or even assert that people are born masters and bondsmen. In religion, he will emphasize that the system of being sat upon is ordained by the divine, is in fact an expression of the divine, or an attribute of original sin, or that those who endure earthily travails will get their reward in the afterlife. The bondsman, unless he has imbibed and accepted the master's view of reality, will have a different take on the entire arrangement: its nature, history, morality, ethics, and aesthetics. In America, for instance, the slave had a different take on whatever the master said and did. Native peoples have a fundamentally different and opposed view of nature and of every historical landmark—following the settlement and colonial period—from that of those who came, conquered, and settled. Questions of illegal and legal immigration have different resonances. I sit on a man's back and persuade him that I am doing everything necessary for him except for getting off his back, said Tolstoy. The persuasion lies in the education system. Whether the situation of the rider and the horse continues and in what form may depend on the extent to which the rider is able to convince the sat-upon of that view, through the content, form, and organization of knowledge.

Once again, the colony provides the best instance of the master's education program and his packaging of knowledge. Colonialism is a practice of power, mostly of a foreign nation over another previously sovereign people, and Fanon aptly described it as a rule of violence where the policeman and the soldier are the daily visible official spokespeople of the colonial state. It is also a social engineering in the sense of breaking up and reordering social and territorial formations, reconstituting them as new societies in redrawn boundaries, with forced allegiance to the foreign flag. The various nation states of Africa today—even their names—were constituted by colonialism in most cases.

Colonialism was also a production of knowledge. Every colonial expedition produced diarists, log keepers, cartographers, and ethnographers who brought back to Europe descriptions of new peoples, geographies, ecologies, plant life, and customs. Their stories, however inadequate and distorted by the need to shock the reader back home, became primary sources and a basis for more speculation and eventual codification and categorization of the new knowledge—for instance the birth of anthropology in the eighteenth century, or even earlier as indicated in the title of Margaret Hodges's *Early Anthropology in the Sixteenth and Seventeenth Centuries* (1964). They affected the history of ideas, including the Enlightenment. Enlightenment, after all, assumes darkness as its other. And the darker the other, the more visible and luminous the light from the European stars. The book *Race and the Enlightenment*, edited by Emmanuel Chukwudi Eze, contains primary documents by the leading lights of the Enlightenment, that reveal how geography and anthropology affected their definition and understanding of reason, prompting Eze in another paper to write about the color of reason.[3] Emmanuel Kant was a teacher of new geography and anthropology, devoting twice as much time and twice as many courses to them as he did to any other subject, including logic. And since he never left Königsberg, his place of birth, he could only have based his knowledge on explorer narratives, ethnographies, and their description of fauna and flora. David Hume's view of the Africans as being naturally inferior to whites, there being "no ingenious manufactures amongst them, no arts, no sciences,"[4] or Hegel's philosophical rhapsodies on the triumphant march of reason in history, somehow bypassing Africa, as well as his negative comments on African religions, were based on the same missionary and explorer narratives. Many of these philosophers used each other as sources and proofs of their own observations; prejudice thus reinforcing prejudice till it became an accepted truth, an authoritative norm. Eze concluded: "Enlightenment philosophy was instrumental in codifying and institutionalizing both the scientific and popular perceptions of the human race."[5]

The scientific and the popular came together in mutual reinforcement in the displays and performance of the African in museums and zoological gardens. Such were the notorious cases of Saartjie Baartman (London, 1801)—the Hottentot Venus of European imagination—and Ota Benga, from the Congo, who were displayed in cages and, in Ota's case, forced to hold monkey babies in his hands. Museums, exhibition halls, zoological cages, and gardens become a performance space, the best example of organizing space to control ways of knowing by ostensibly offering evidence and proof.

In her groundbreaking work *Destination Culture*, which explores the staging of tourism, museums and heritage, Barbara Kirshenblatt-Gimblett aptly pointed out the role of such performance space in blurring the line between the apparently weighty and the visibly popular: "The inherently performative nature of live specimens veers exhibits of them strongly in the direction of spectacle, blurring still further the line between morbid curiosity and scientific interest, chamber of horrors and medical exhibition, circus and zoological garden, theater and living ethnographic display, scholarly lecture and dramatic monologue, cultural performance and stage re-creation."[6]

Professor Patricia Penn Hilden has written of how ethnographic museums have often shaped the view of indigenous peoples. In her paper "Race for Sale: Narratives of Possession in Two 'Ethnic' Museums,"[7] she showed how the displays of Native Americans in museums, in the very act of dislocation and relocation, decontexting and recontexting, ends up in distortions.

Such zoos and ethnographic museums played a role in popularizing and invigorating interest in the colonially originated discipline of anthropology and cultural geography and no doubt also enhanced the standing of their intellectuals as authorities on Africa.

Intellectuals of the European Enlightenment and their work came to occupy center stage in a vast echo chamber. For one, they held powerful positions in their different academies and, apart from their mutual intertextuality,[8] they would pass their unified perspective to their students who would of course pass it on till it became a tradition, an inheritable truth. In 1960, with many African countries independent or on the verge of independence, a disciple of Hegel, Trevor Roper, could assert, as the new Chair of History at Oxford, that Africa was only darkness prior to European presence; and as darkness was not a subject of history, Africa's real history began with European presence. This becomes the general self-image of the colonizer (the master) vis-à-vis the colonized as the alpha of the human epoch, completely blind to the fact that the colonial bondsman had an independent history prior to their contact and trial by death. Fanon summarized this self-image of the master as the maker of history vis-à-vis the colonized: "And because he constantly refers to the history of his mother country, he clearly indicates that he himself is the extension of that mother country. Thus the history which he writes is not the history of the country which he plunders but the history of his own nation in regard to all that she skims off, all that she violates and starves."[9]

When such ideas become popularized in fiction, stories, and film, from Rider Haggard of *King Solomon's Mines* to *Avatar*, they percolate through society and become an integral part of the general consciousness as a view of the other and his environment. The image of the other as bystanders in a history that passes them by can be imbibed even by some of the colonized and their natural allies. Image is more powerful than logic and demonstrable facts.

I am not even talking about the past or the consciously prejudiced. In February 2010, I went to read from my novel *Wizard of the Crow* in Fort Collins, Colorado, where I met an African-American lady doing great work with orphaned children in Kampala, Uganda. As I had lived in Uganda for five years in the 1950s, I was happy to go down memory lane. I wanted to know about the current state of Kampala and Makerere, my alma mater. Had her parents been to visit her in Kampala? She started laughing. Apparently, they were scared of crossing paths with dangerous animals in the streets and no amount of pictures of the city built on seven hills, like Rome, would disabuse them of their perception. That was an African-American couple. In 2003, a year after I came to Irvine, a white lady and her son came to see me at my home in University Hills because her son had chosen Kenya for his project. My chance to catch them young, I thought, and I did everything I could to educate him about Kenya. I had two copies of a glossy magazine, a special issue on Kenya. I showed him pictures of the skyscrapers in Nairobi; Mombasa Beach Hotels by the blue waters; suburban residential houses really no different from the gated communities of Irvine; giraffes, zebras, lions and rhinos roaming the wild; Maasai herdsmen and their cattle in the plains. I also pointed at pictures of city slums and rural dwellings of grass thatch and iron roofs. All this was Kenya, I told him, modern Kenya. Poverty and opulence walked hand in hand in the streets. I gave him a copy of the magazine and told him he could cut and paste. When later I heard from his mother that he and his group had received an A for the project, I was quite excited, almost patting myself on my good work; I looked forward to seeing it. Well, there was not a single picture of Nairobi skyscrapers, suburbs, beach hotels, traffic jams, or street lights. But there were plenty of pictures of wild life, Maasai herdsmen in the plains, and slums. The Kenya of modern highways, cars, trains, and airports had been left out of a Kenya of fauna, flora, and slums. Both couples, it must be noted, identified with Africa; the first, because of their daughter, and the second, because it was their chosen subject for their project. But they clearly had a deep-rooted view of the continent that could not be shaken by any evidence to the contrary or that complicated the perceived notion of the continent. In his autobiography, Sidney Poitier describes his first visit to Africa. He stayed in a modern hotel in South Africa. But he admits that he caught himself checking for snakes under the bed. He was trying to demonstrate that such a simplified view of Africa could not have come from a consciously held negative bias: it had been the result of years and years of propagation of a certain kind of knowledge about the continent and its history. It was still the Africa of Hegel.

Unfortunately, this "knowledge" did not remain in Europe. A multitude of teachers would later export the intellectual greats of Europe and their learned conclusions and attitudes to the colonial classroom. It was not a question of inadequate or deliberate distortion of knowledge. The exporters did not say one thing in the classroom and then write another in their books and scholarly papers, or, for that matter, teach different physics, biology, and chemistry. Some had high international visibility and often received good positions when they returned to their countries. In fact, in the case of East Africa, the colleges were initially affiliated to the University of London, and the degree certificate was that of London. I believe that most teachers in schools and colleges, as I am trying to show in my memoirs, were sincere, dedicated, desirous of conveying the truth, and would eschew the more populist simplistic views. But that truth had already been infused with attitudes and assumptions that placed Europe as the beginning of history and knowledge. The very order of knowledge, what is included and left out of the curriculum, reinforced the view that Europe was the center of the universe. Any theater or film director or painter will tell you that the organization of space, be it the stage, the museum, the screen, or the canvas, conveys meaning. Whether in Michelangelo's "Last Judgment" on the ceiling of the Sistine Chapel or Leonardo Da Vinci's "The Last Supper," there are centers of power, around which the figures are organized. The power relationship is suggested by their placement in the space relative to other placements. In the Department of Performance Studies at New York University, I used to teach a popular course on the politics of performance space, where we looked at the spatial organization of power in sports fields, theaters, museums, and even the streets. The paper based on those seminars later became part of my 1996 Clarendon lectures at Oxford, which were published by Oxford University Press as *Penpoints, Gunpoints, and Dreams.* The spatial and temporal organization of knowledge can be an expression of power relationship, consciously or unconsciously intended.

We can take the example of English literature in the colony. India was the major English imperial center from where many social experiments were exported to other British possessions. In Kenya, for instance, the Indian penal code was applied almost intact in the administration of law and justice. So we can take the thinking behind the establishment of English education, literature in particular, as generally applicable to their later exports to Africa. The advocates saw the export in terms of ideology, idealism, and unmitigated intellectual jingoism. The often quoted "Minutes on Indian Education" by Thomas Babington Macaulay (member of the Supreme Court of India, 1834–38) combines all those elements in his advocacy of such an education. It was pure jingoism in his declaration that English stood "pre-eminent even among the languages of the west."[10] The export of English was a kind of prophetic fulfillment of the words of the sixteenth-century poet Samuel Daniel, who had envisioned the possibility of the new assertive English emerging from the shadow of Latin, later becoming an export commodity to other realms. He asks, who knows,

> . . . to what strange shores
> This gaine of our best glory shall be sent
> T'inrich unknowing Nations with our stores?
> What worlds in th'yet unformed Occident
> May come refin'd with th' accents that are ours?[11]

But the point is that the other imperial nations—France, Portugal, and Spain, for instance—would have made similar claims of superiority about their own linguistic, literary, and pedagogical export. Beyond national jingoism, Macaulay's was also a paternalistic argument against the Indian system of education. The Indians were to be taught what was best to know. English was better to know than Sanskrit or Arabic, he said, believing it no exaggeration to say "that all the historical information which has been collected from all the books written in Sanskrit languages is less valuable than what may be found in the most paltry abridgement used in preparatory schools in England."[12]

Macaulay even mocks the Indian system as teaching children only how to wash their hands after touching a goat. Today, even if one were to concede that the English language and all the content it carried were essential for Indian modernization, it can be pointed out that Japan and China did not go the way of English language and literature. But Macaulay would not have heeded this, for in the "Minutes" he is quite open about descending from the heights of idealism and altruism to the ideological, asserting the aim of their education as being to create "a class of Indians, Indian in blood and color, but English in taste, in opinions, in morals, and in intellect," but with a very practical end, that this class may be "interpreters between us and the millions whom we govern."[13]

That is precisely the point. It is less the content of what's taught or even how it is taught than the power relationship between the Indian and the English system. Shakespeare's poems and plays do not lose their beauty and dramatic content for being taught by an English expatriate to colonial subjects, but the placement in the curriculum, the space Shakespeare occupies relative to others—whether, for instance, he is the only dramatist taught—can tell a tale beyond the text. Macaulay is clear that English must occupy the center, or rather the base, that was previously the domain of the Indian system. Between the two systems is a struggle to death to establish who is the master. The Indian system must die to make possible the life of the English system. The struggle unto death that Hegel talks about is everything and involves all levels of power. As Frantz Fanon put it, "Colonialism is not satisfied merely with holding a people in its grip and emptying the native's brains of all form and content. By a kind of perverted logic, it turns to the past of oppressed people, and distorts, disfigures, and destroys it."[14] Your past must give way to my past, your literature must give way to my literature, my way is the high way, in fact the only way.

In Macaulayism, we are witnessing the master's colonization of the cognitive base and process. A child beginning to walk takes one step, then another, adding new knowledge to the previous one, but continually returning to the base, his mother, the starting point. Not only a child: we all add new knowledge to what we already have. The Chinese saying that a journey of a thousand miles begins with one step is also true of pedagogical and intellectual journeys. The step begins on the ground where one stands. The colonial process dislocates the traveler's mind from the place he or she already knows to a foreign starting point even with the body still remaining in his or her homeland. It is a process of continuous alienation from the base, a continuous process of looking at oneself from the outside of self or with the lenses of a stranger. One may end up identifying with the foreign base as the starting point toward self, that is from another self toward oneself, rather than the local being the starting point, from self to other selves. Instead of a journey from Sanskrit to the English script, it is the other way round, from the English script to the Sanskrit. But most times there is not even a Sanskrit to return to, even for comparative purposes—it may have been destroyed. Or, if still present, there may not be any returners: one may have been deracinated from the base beyond repair; the alienation from the base may have gone beyond the point of a desire to return.

This colonization of the cognitive process was the everyday experience in a colonial classroom anywhere. In the secondary school phase of the memoirs I am currently writing, I am recording the same story: English language, literature, history, and geography first. Any Kenyan of my generation will tell you that they knew many natural, historical landmarks of London they had never seen long before they knew a single street of their capital, let alone the major rivers of their country. In the words of Edward Blyden, the great nineteenth-century African educator of Afro-Caribbean origins, "they sung of their history, which was the history of our degradation. They recited their triumphs which contained the records of our humiliation. To our great misfortune, we learned their prejudices and their passions, and thought we had their aspirations and their power."[15] Blyden, who had already returned to Africa, his life astride free Liberia and colonial Sierra Leone, was writing in 1883 about the education of Africans in West Africa. He talks of a child who initially revolts from colonial views of his history and culture but later accepts them as proper because of their repetition in newspapers and books: "Having embraced, or at least assented, to these errors and falsehoods about himself, he concludes that his only hope of rising in the scale of respectable manhood is to strive after whatever is most unlike himself and most alien to his tastes."[16]

This, of course, is one response to the master's education of the bondsman: accept his view of history and work within its premises. This, in fact, is the response of the other bondsman in the pairings of Shakespeare's *The Tempest*. When Ariel, returning from a mission accomplished, asks Prospero for the liberty he had promised in exchange for loyal service without lies, grudges, or errors, Prospero is angry and reminds Ariel of the past from which his art had freed him. Ariel's response is apologetic and grateful: that's so my noble master. What shall I do?

This is in contrast to Caliban's response to Prospero's narrative of the past, asserting his own sovereignty prior to the contact between them. As for the language imposed, he uses it to curse Prospero's art and view of history. In his rewrite of the play under the title *A Tempest* (1968), Césaire clarifies Caliban's revolt:

> Prospero, you're a great magician:
> you're an old hand at deception.
> And you have lied to me so much,
> about the world, about myself,
> that you ended up by imposing on me
> an image of myself:
> underdeveloped, in your words, undercompetent
> that's how you made me see myself!
> And I hate that image . . . and it's false!
> But now I know you, you old cancer,
> And I also know myself![17]

It's interesting that Caliban, in both Shakespeare and Césaire, answers Prospero in Prospero's language, which takes us to the second phase of Hegel's dialect. The bondsman knows the master in a way that the master does not know him. He knows the language and the culture that's being imposed on him, but the master does not know the tongue of the bondsman and the culture it carries. He does not think it has anything to offer because he has already condemned it as not being human. Caliban's self-consciousness is clearly impacted by his awareness of Prospero's language and the world it carries. Caliban is on firmer and broader ground in rejecting Prospero's narrative of history. Du Bois' celebrated notion of double consciousness, which he saw as residing and warring in the soul of the African American, becomes a unified consciousness in the aesthetics of resistance. He is an inheritor of two worlds.

African literature, even that in European languages, starts with that rejection of the master's narrative of history. This is best summarized by Chinua Achebe in his statement that if he were God he "would regard as the worst, our acceptance, for whatever reason of our racial inferiority,"[18] and that he would be satisfied if his art, at the very least, succeeded in teaching his African readers "that their past—with all its imperfections—was not one long night of savagery from which the first Europeans acting on God's behalf delivered them."[19] Frantz Fanon underlined the same view when he wrote that "in the psycho-affective equilibrium," the claim to a past was responsible for an important change in the colonized. It rehabilitated the nation and served "as a justification for the hope of a future national culture."[20]

The literature, simultaneously a rejection of the master's view and an affirmation of the native voice, was a manifesto of that change in the colonized: would it become or at least justify the hope for a new culture? On the contrary, it was the colonial order of knowledge, as in the Nairobi of the sixties that was now forming the postcolonial literary intellectual. It reflected the general situation. The national army and police force was the same colonial military and police force that had been deployed against Kenyan nationalism for sixty years. The judicial system, now national, was the same as existed in the colonial era. The economic process of the export of raw material and import of finished products, the price of both still determined by Europe, prevailed.

There was something familiar about this. I had read it in Fanon's *The Wretched of the Earth*, where he discusses the nature of the middle class that takes power at the end of the colonial regime in terms of its economic, intellectual, and cultural poverty and ultimately lack of a vision that would set the newly independent country on a new footing. This is because of the mimic character of the national bourgeoisie that "identifies itself with the western bourgeoisie, from whom it has learnt its lessons."[21] A conglomeration of all these factors, "the economic channels of the young state sink back inevitably into neocolonialist lines."[22] It was as if Fanon had been born and raised in Kenya. The order of knowledge assumed by the English Department as then organized was in tune with the general neocolonial content of the newly independent state.

The document, "On the Abolition of the English Department," was not a call for retreat and isolation, it was a plea for the decolonization of the cognitive process. On looking back now, I can see that it was doing something more. The document was also questioning, even attacking, the study of literature within purely national boundaries, or rather criticizing the intellectual self-enclosure of the exclusive study of a national literature, the more so because in our case it was not even our own national literature. It was a foreign national literature wearing the mask of universality.

There was this ironic twist in the emergent reality, a little reminiscent of that of dependent master and independent bondsman in Hegel's dialect: a sense of universality was actually the foundation of the new literature, and it was so precisely because it was a product of the struggle of the double consciousness inherent in the education of the colonial bondsman, now unified in resistance. Even if they wanted, the writers from the colony could not divest themselves of the literature and culture they had imbibed in the master's classroom. Aimé Césaire admitted his roots in surrealism, Andre Breton, the guru of the movement, wrote a preface to Césaire's *Return to My Native Land*. Surrealism led him to Africa, to his negritude, buried beneath the surface of his French education and cultural assimilation. A Wole Soyinka could not write as if he had not read the Bible, studied Greek and Latin classics, wrestled with Ben Jonson and Shakespeare, and communed with the Anglo-Irish. At the same time, the Yoruba pantheon infuses his work. In his work, the Yoruba, the Judeo-Graeco-Latin, and the Anglo-Irish are unified in a new synthesis. Achebe's titles, like *Things Fall Apart* and *No Longer at Ease*, are homages to the writer's intellectual formation. The title of my first published novel, *Weep Not Child*, was taken from Walt Whitman. Some of these phrases have become part of the intellectual everyday in Africa. But even beyond the titles, the intertextuality of Europhone African literature with the European is remarkable. Sembene Ousmane's great novel *God's Bits of Wood* has strong affinities with Emile Zola's *Germinal*, and my own *A Grain of Wheat* with Joseph Conrad's *Under Western Eyes*. I used to teach Achebe's *Things Fall Apart* alongside Thomas Hardy's *The Mayor of Casterbridge* and Sophocles' *Oedipus*. Okot p'Bitek wrote his very African poem, "Song of Lawino," after he had read Longfellow's "Song of Hiawatha." He first wrote it in his mother tongue before rendering it into English. But here there is no welcome for missionaries. Lawino, the woman narrator, castigates her husband for abandoning the ways of his people, comparable to a Minnehaha castigating a Hiawatha. And yet these literary products were not derivatives. They are a synthesis forged in resistance. Without resistance there is no motion. The resulting synthesis, whether in Africa, Asia, or Latin America, speaks to Africa, the formerly colonized, and the world.

Our Nairobi document called for a reordering of the process of knowing and specifically for placing the new synthesis of African, Caribbean, African-American literature and the kindred literatures of Asia and Latin America at a center of a new order of knowing, and then European Literature being brought in at the edges, however centered in its own places. In short, it called for centering the postcolonial in the world of knowing.

GLOBALECTICAL IMAGINATION

The World in the Postcolonial

It was the German poet and dramatist Goethe who wrote that there was no such thing as patriotic art or science: both belong, like all good things, to the whole world.[1] One of the earliest to talk of a possible world literature, he said that it could be fostered only by an untrammeled intercourse among all contemporaries, bearing in mind "what we have inherited from the past."[2] That was in 1801, in his journal *Propyläen*. By January 1827 he was convinced that such world literature was actually in the process of being constituted, which would lead him to assert, in the same month, that "national literature is now a rather unmeaning term; the epoch of world literature is at hand, and everyone must strive to hasten its approach."[3] For almost thirty years, between 1801 and 1831, in different fora, and in almost identical wording, he continued to restate that conviction.

Germany was not yet a colony-owning imperial nation and Goethe may have been thinking of Europe, but still, his position contrasts dramatically with the 1835 Macaulayan advocacy of English language and literature as a superior replacement of Indian heritage, in fact more valuable than the other contemporary European cultures. Part of what gave Goethe confidence in the imminence of his *Weltliteratur* was what he saw in 1828 as a "greater ease of communication."[4] He also talked of the exchange of journals as enabling a shared heritage of the best of the European nations. Translation was the major means of mutual enrichment, and he described it as giving new life, in a foreign language, to a text that had lost luster in the original because of overfamiliarity through overusage. Though obviously responding to developments in Europe, the ease of communication for instance, Goethe was expressing a subjective desire that could be hastened by actions of intellectuals.

It was Marx and Engels who articulated the objective material and historical basis for such a world literature in their communist manifesto of 1848. Its possibility or, for them, logical inevitability was inherent in the dramatic development of capitalism. From its emergence into dominance in the social process in the fifteenth and sixteenth century in its mercantile stage, capitalism always had a globalizing tendency, noted by Adam Smith in *The Wealth of Nations* and, after him, Marx in *Das Capital*. For Smith, looking back from 1776, "The discovery of America and that of a passage to the East Indies by the Cape of Good Hope, are the two greatest and most important events recorded in the history of mankind. Their consequences have already been very great."[5]

Marx and Engels merely elaborate on these consequences when, looking back from 1848, they say that

> the discovery of gold and silver in America, the extirpation, enslavement and entombment in mines of the aboriginal population, the beginning of the conquest and looting of the East Indies, the turning of Africa into a warren for the commercial hunting of black-skins, signalized the rosy dawn of the era of capitalist production. These idyllic proceedings are the chief momenta of primitive accumulation. On their heels treads the commercial war of the European nations, with the globe for a theatre.[6]

By the time they wrote this, capital had evolved from the mercantile to its industrial stage. The slave plantation system as the way of organizing labor for maximum yield had been replaced by the factory system; the slave was no good for the factory. The slave was replaced by the wage earner. Within Europe, or England, the early home of the industrial revolution, the wage earner came from the victims of the enclosure movement, driven by necessity from the country to the factory. Trade in humans is replaced by industrial products. The factory does not gorge on human labor only, but on natural resources as well. The import of raw materials and export of finished goods are the imperatives of the new industrial capital.

So Marx and Engels would observe correctly that raw materials for national industries were "drawn from the remotest zones; industries whose products are consumed, not only at home, but in every quarter of the globe. In place of the old wants, satisfied by the production of the country, we find new wants, requiring for their satisfaction the products of distant lands and climes. In place of the old local and national seclusion and self-sufficiency, we have intercourse in every direction, universal inter-dependence of nations."[7]

The universal interdependence in the reign of industrial capital that they talked about in 1848 has become globalization, the global reign of financial capital. The cheap prices of the factory-produced commodities they saw as the heavy artillery that battered all national walls has been replaced by financial capital that has come to break all national barriers in its movement across the globe. The international financial institutions, the IMF and World Bank for instance, have come to determine the economic policies of many nations; they constitute what, in my novel *Wizard of the Crow*, I described as the Global Ministry of Finance. If nineteenth-century interdependence was facilitated by the vastly improved means of communications, twentieth- and twenty-first-century globalization and the movement of financial capital in and out of national boundaries is made possible by an intensified communication system that has increased a thousandfold, making ordinary Hamlet's words to his friend that there were more things in heaven and earth than were dreamt of in Horatio's philosophy.

Indeed by road, sea, air, and even space, every corner of the globe is connected, consolidating the global character of production, exchange, and consumption. Information technology (internet, fax, emails, texting, Facebook, YouTube, etc.) has turned our planet into a neighborhood, or what Goethe called an expanded homeland and McLuhan a global village. Disasters or triumphs in one part of the globe can be witnessed in real time in every other part. A book with translations can be simultaneously published in all the capitals of the globe: witness the lines that awaited, say, the publication of the Harry Potter series, from Europe to Japan! The journals that Goethe talked about, not to mention books, music, and images, can be downloaded from every corner of the world instantly. The e-book is more instant than instant coffee. International conferences, real or virtual, are the order of the day. The old long-distance learning through written correspondence has been overtaken by online learning. A teacher anywhere in the world can have students from all corners of the globe attending his lectures virtually at the same time.

In the midst of writing this book, I got an email from Mr. David Homa, a teacher at Los Gatos High School near San Jose. He wrote in regard to teaching my fiction in the Millennium Villages School2School program, started in 2009 by the Millennium Promise Organization in collaboration with the Earth Institute at Columbia University and the Whitby School in Greenwich, Connecticut. "My anthropology and economics classes," he wrote to me,

> have been "going to school" with students at Kisumu Day High School in Kisumu, Kenya. We have been using the internet and Skype to do cross-curricular activities. The past few weeks students from both schools have been reading *The River Between*. After the students read sections of the book we then have a Skype call so all the students can discuss what they have read. It has been amazing to watch students on different sides of the world speak with each other in real time and discuss your book. It certainly is giving my students a very unique and eye opening experience about Kenyan culture.

This experience, clearly part of what's going in the world, is dramatically captured in a Cisco commercial where a visitor to a school in the United States is welcomed into the class by students proclaiming that they are going to China. The visitor can only react with envy as she remembers that the furthest place her class ever visited when she was a student was a neighborhood farm. But it turns out that

China is closer than even the neighborhood farm as the camera opens and the children in China and America raise their hands in greetings to one another in real time.

The fact is, the virtual learning system and institutions of the publishing house, the bookshop, and the classroom have arrived and are molding the global intellectual climate. Goethe and Marx foresaw a reality that is now unfolding. The invisible world dreamt up by H. G. Wells in his *Invisible Man* is here. This virtual world is producing the third order of Adam, cyberture, after nurture and nature, which is able to cross the barriers of time and space in seconds. Most affected is the movement of ideas.

Marx and Engels could have been describing today, but more accurately, when they wrote that the international dependence of their time in material production was also reflected in intellectual production, concluding, à la Goethe, that "the intellectual creations of individual nations become common property. National one-sidedness and narrow-mindedness become more and more impossible, and from the numerous national and local literatures, there arises a world literature."[8]

World literature is here: unfortunately, it has not meant the end of national one-sidedness and narrow-mindedness. On the contrary it often has been viewed with such one-sidedness and narrow-mindedness. Since first articulated by Goethe, the term has intrigued scholars and has been revisited many times to break down the one-sidedness and narrow-mindedness of its viewing to release its true worldliness.[9] In recent years this interest has intensified with courses in world literature in various institutions. There have also been anthologies of world literature even though there are questions of their representativeness. I have seen literature texts in some Irvine schools that, though thin in some areas in terms of their world spread, are a far cry from the Eurocentric blindness of yesterday. The discussions and theorizing generated by the term have touched on issues of definition, inclusion, organization, and approaches, the totality of packaging for classroom delivery.

In attempts to define and capture the Goethian essence, terms to describe it have ranged from Richard Green Mouton's "autobiography of civilization"[10] to Pascale Casanova's "The World Republic of Letters."[11] But no term can really substitute for the one coined by Goethe. World literature must include what's already formed in the world as well as what's now informed by the world, at once a coalition, a cohesion, and coalescence of literatures in world languages into global consciousness. It is a process.

At present, the postcolonial is the closest to that Goethian and Marxian conception of world literature because it is a product of different streams and influences from different points of the globe, a diversity of sources, which it reflects in turn. The postcolonial is inherently outward looking, inherently international in its very constitution in terms of themes, language, and the intellectual formation of the writers. It would be quite productive to look at world literature, though not exclusively, through postcoloniality.

The term *postcolonial*, however, is problematic, despite its widespread use as description and theory. As a periodization, it raises more questions than it answers. Periodization of any sort, in science or history, as Tim Reiss has warned,[12] is wrought with conflicting histories, geographies, ideologies, and perspectives, depending on who—where, when, and how—is setting the differentiating markers of events and time. However, that of the postcolonial is even more elusive as a settled marker. It could refer to the period after the act and fact of colonization. Is the colonial period that follows the act also postcolonial? Can you then have postcolonial colonialism? This raises the specter of countless *posts*. Or does it refer exclusively to the period after the rupture with imperial Europe, the independence era, deemed the formal end of colonialism, the after-the-end of colonialism? It could apply to the whole planet, in the sense of a precolonial, colonial, and postcolonial world, including the West of course, as when we say B.C. and A.D., before and after the Christian era. In this case does it replace or absorb the terms modern and postmodern as a reference to the same historical periods? As K. Anthony Appiah has asked, "Is the post- in postmodernism the post- in post-colonial?"[13]

Conceptually, it could refer to any situation where colonialism or similar forms of domination is followed by liberation or independence no matter when this happened, and thus assume that the postcolonial could be used to refer to periods before the times of its currently assumed reference. In that sense, the emergence of European nations from the medieval world, dominated by Catholicism and Latin, could be a postcolonial period. In such a scenario, a country can have as many postcolonial moments as it has been colonized by other peoples. Britain, for instance, would have at least two postcolonial moments, the post-Roman and post-Norman colonial. What about the postcolonial of the colonizing? Every postcolonial, as periodization, must carry the *posts* of the colonizer and colonized, and they can't very well mean the same thing.

The question is complicated by the fact that there were colonialisms within colonialism, the prime example being America, where European settler colonists felt colonized by the mother countries and revolted, in most cases actually fighting for their independence, but the colonization of indigenous peoples by those of Europe remained unresolved, or rather made permanent by the very victories of the settler-child against the mother. The unresolved internal colonialism also remains in countries like Australia, New Zealand, Canada, and throughout Latin America where the original colonized indigenous peoples never went through an independence stage. Have they gone through a postcolonial period? The postcoloniality of the indigenous cannot be identical with that of the settling communities.

As a conceptual term it raises the question as to whether there are features common to any postcolonial condition that would enable its easy identification as such. This could make the term a tool of analysis like Marxism, which has been used to study precapitalist social formations before Marx, for instance in George D. Thompson's study of ancient Greece.[14] Marxism has been used to open doors into the realms of politics, economy, scholarship, and the studies of power relationships between peoples in the past, centuries before Marx was born. Can the postcolonial be used in the same way to help extend the knowledge of areas and relationships in times past? There are other concerns: such as that the term *postcolonial* gives the impression that colonialism, its content and form, is something of the past. Whenever I have given courses in postcolonial theories and narratives, I always devote one seminar to the neo-in-the-post of postcolonialism. Neocolonialism is not simply a continuation of the colonial, but it carries the sense of the continuities of colonial structures in changed political forms. It also raises the possibility of a country that was not a colony being dominated in a manner that has all the features of the neocolonial, for instance Eastern European nations vis-à-vis their dominant Western partners; or the possibility that neocolonial relationships are developed not with the old colonial powers but with new ones—for instance, the Latin American colonial relationship with Europe mutating into a neocolonial relationship with the more powerful north. The neocolonial is an important feature, though not necessarily the sole defining feature, of the postcolonial.

Whatever questions the term raises, as a concept or simply as a marker of periods, it has one constant: the *post* expresses a relationship to coloniality, in fact it absorbs the colonial into itself. In so doing, it simultaneously assumes a relationship to something else that is neither colonial nor postcolonial. This other, the noncolonial, takes itself as the mainstream, and tends to see coloniality and everything emerging from it, even if it is a *post*, as somehow peripheral to its self-perception as the sole embodiment of continuity and maker of modernity and history of ideas. But this is simply the master's narrative of history as we have seen in the four pairings in Shakespeare, Defoe, Hegel, and Fanon. The narrative of a mainstream versus a colonial periphery has been contested even within those pairings.

In their struggle, the imperial lord and the colonial bondsman leave marks on each other, but with the difference that the bondsman can appropriate the best of the imperial input and combine it with the best of his own into a new synthesis that assumes the "globe for a theatre." The postcolonial embodies this new synthesis. While having its own particularity, like all other tributaries to the human, the postcolonial is an integral part of the intellectual history of the modern world because its very coloniality is a history of interpenetration of different peoples, cultures, and knowledge.

Colonialism and its aftermath has been characterized by the movement of peoples, migrations from places of native origins into others' places. First was the voluntary and involuntary movement to lands that already belonged to indigenous peoples. The voluntary was that of European peoples to form the old settler colonies of the Americas, and later Australia, and New Zealand. The involuntary was the movement of African peoples, as slaves, to provide labor in these colonies, or later the movement of Asians, though not in the same way as enslaved peoples, as indentured labor. Modern America was the result of the interpenetration of three continents: Africa, indigenous America, and Europe, however unequal the basis and the process. Australia and New Zealand were similarly the results of the intermingling of Europe and native peoples (aboriginals, Maoris, etc). There was similar intermingling in the settler colonies of Africa. Even the protectorates, the purely commercial colonies in Africa and Asia, brought in military, administrative, and spiritual engineers to ensure that capital was not challenged or resisted by indigenous peasant, feudal, or semifeudal organizations of labor. In sum, Europe was able to export its peoples to the other four continents of Africa, Asia, America, and Australia in a way that no other continent had ever done.

Arising from this movement of peoples was an intermingling of cultures, however unequal. The spread of European languages to other continents was the most salient of European cultural exports, central to the structure of the lord's education of the colonial bondsman. Domination and resistance traditions were largely expressed and negotiated in European languages. The colony was a meeting of cultures, histories, and cosmic views. The cultures impacted each other to produce a third, the modern, bearing the marks of many streams, giving what Marx called a "cosmopolitan character" to cultural exchange.[15] From its very inception, the colony was the real depository of the cosmopolitan.

There is a second phase in the movement of peoples. Where in the heyday of imperialism, movement was largely from Europe to other continents, after the Second World War and into independence and now globalization, there have been migrations from Asia, Africa, and the Pacific to the original "mother" countries, or to Western metropolises in general, bringing into them the cosmopolitan character of colonial being. Again, this was also a movement of cultures and ideas.

The East African Asian who went to Europe, Canada, and America after their expulsion from Uganda by Idi Amin brought with them a heritage of cultural streams from Asia and Africa. Most of their parents and grandparents had originally emigrated from Southeast Asia to East Africa for a variety of historical reasons; they were part of the evolution of the modern East African cultures. In terms of migration of ideas, a good example is the birth of *Transition* magazine. The journal, founded in the early sixties and edited by Rajat Neogy, whose birth, upbringing, and entire schooling was in Kampala, became synonymous with the birth of the postcolonial African intellectual. It opened its pages to such luminaries, then in their youth, as Ali Mazrui, Wole Soyinka, and Peter Nazareth, and featured the 1962 conference of writers of English expression. When Neogy moved to America, his journal went with him, from Ghana to Harvard. It has been going strong ever since, fifty years now. A French-language parallel is the Paris-based *Presence Africaine*, founded by the Senegalese Alioune Diop even before *Transition*.

Another example, already cited, was the great wave of Caribbean peoples migrating to England in the fifties in search of what George Lamming, in his great novel *The Emigrants*, described as a better break. Largely a workers' migration, it was also one of intellectuals, and it produced the Caribbean literary renaissance that gave to the world of letters George Lamming, Samuel Selvon, and V. S. Naipaul among others.

Whether at home or in the metropolis, European languages became the common means of intellectual production, blurring what is metropolitan and colonial in origins. Blurred too is the question of definition and identity. When Asians and Africans write in English, their product is surely part of English language cultural universe. Can this writing be defined within a purely national boundary? Is Naipaul a Caribbean or an English writer? Does Salman Rushdie belong to Europe or Asia? The same goes for French, Spanish, and Portuguese. Senghor and Césaire belong to the French literary tradition as much as they do to that of their African and Martiniquan roots. Senghor was the head of state of a foreign French colony, Senegal, and yet ended up as a member of the prestigious French Academy. Similarly, Agostinho Neto and Pepetela belong to the Portuguese language system as much as they belong to their Angolan roots, and the question of whether they should be defined as Angolan or Portuguese writers or both applies. The three Nobelites, Nadine Gordimer, Wole Soyinka, and J. M. Coetzee, by virtue of their common usage of English, must belong to the English language community as much as Assia Djebar and Senghor belong to the French language community. The new generation of European-born writers, children of immigrants, bring into their work the heritage of their parents with roots in the different cultures of the globe. Even within Europe, children of immigrants from Eastern Europe, Turkey included, are doing the same. They bring globality into their Western European experience.

The United States offers a significant example of the postcolonial as the site of globality. There is no community, language, or religion anywhere in the globe that has no presence in the United States. They come practically from all the corners of the globe and they bring into their U.S. experience what they have absorbed from their heritage. Their cultures have contributed to what's called "American." U.S. literature as much as its music and performance is not just European. It is also African, Asian, and Pacific. The rainbow literature and culture that result from migrations to the North is being replicated in the West generally. But the same phenomenon is to be found in all cultures and countries impacted by the imperial center. So no matter the definition, it is clear that globality as much as coloniality are the constant features in the postcolonial even when the latter refers exclusively to those societies and peoples impacted by imperial colonialism.

Outside the fact of language, writers from the colonial world always assumed an extranational dimension. We talk of African literature, for instance, without batting an eyelid. Africa is one of the largest continents in the world, containing within it, in terms of geographic space or land mass, Europe, North America, Australia, and China combined. In terms of nations, Africa has more than fifty. But African literature always saw itself as beyond the national territorial state, assuming, at the minimum, the continent for its theater of relevance and application.

The negritude literary movement was not only continentalist, it had inspirational roots and alliances in Afro-Cubanism, Afro-Brazilianism, Haitian Indigenism, and the Harlem Renaissance, thus crossing borders of languages, nations, countries, and continents.

Discussing national culture at the First Congress of Black Artists and Writers in Paris, 1956, Frantz Fanon took the position—later reworked differently by Fredric Jameson in terms of third-world literatures being national allegories—that the literature then produced in Africa was not a national literature but a Negro Literature.

"Colonialism did not dream of wasting its time in denying the existence of one national culture after another. Therefore the reply of the colonized peoples will be straight away continental in its breadth. In Africa, the native literature of the last twenty years is not a national literature but a Negro literature."[16] This is why Frantz Fanon is the original theorist of the postcolonial. The issues he raised, even on literature and culture, took into account the colonized world as a whole, what later bore the name "third world."

In reality the postcolonial is not simply located in the third world. Literally rooted in the intertexuality of products from all the corners of the globe, its universalist tendency is inherent in its very relationship to historical colonialism and its globe for a theater. Jameson's comment that "any conception of world literature necessarily demands some specific engagement with the question of third-world literature"[17] should be amended to say that any such conception must bring the postcolonial to the center. The postcolonial is at the heart of the constitution of Goethe's world literature, and even in theory, it indeed constitutes the nonimperial heart of the modern and postmodern.

In such a world of shared intellectual property, organizing the teaching of literature on the principle of national boundaries is outmoded, and even more so the export of national literatures as a superior knowledge. Goethe advised fellow Germans to look "beyond the narrow circle that surrounds us."[18] He liked to look about himself in foreign nations and he advised everyone to do the same. Goethe and Marx did not see or mean that any one national literature would constitute world literature. World literature would be like the sea or the ocean into which all streams from all corners of the globe would flow. The sea is constituted of many rivers, some of which cross many fields, but the rivers and their constituent streams do not lose their individuality as streams and rivers. The result is the vastness of the sea and the ocean. Confronted with the possibility of that reality, and, quite frankly, its vastness, it is easy for organizers of literary knowledge to stop in fright and stay within a national boundary, taking comfort in the certainty of the structures already tried and passed on as tradition. The traditional organization of literature along national boundaries is like bathing in a river instead of sailing in the ocean, or trying to contain a river's flow within a specific territory.

In the case of Nairobi in the sixties, what was needed was the daring arrogance and ignorance of youth to question the given. In the Nairobi debate, we questioned the colonially rooted reversal of the "normal" cognitive process where from "here to there" had been replaced by from "there" only, with the hope that one could see "here" from "there." But we also questioned the cognitive value of studying genres of literature within periods of a single national literature, in our case a foreign one at that, unless of course one wanted to become an expert or an authority on that literature. We had seen the fruitful value of studying drama in its development from the Greeks to Modern Europe. Though generally bound within Europe, the study of drama had been freed from the English national boundary. So, what about the novel? For instance, how could one study the European novel and leave out, say, Tolstoy and Dostoevsky? The language of access was not an issue: after all, the Greek plays studied, in the case of drama, were translations. The change of the name of the department from English to Literature signaled intent: from Kenya, and with African, Caribbean, African-American literatures at the center, we would surely connect with the globe, Western parts of the globe included.

When it came to a working structure we were confronted with the challenges of the vastness. Our option for the generic studies of the novel and drama—their development—and our call for electives in Asian, Latin American, and Euro-American literatures with the possibilities for more depending on resources and demand was part of the response to the challenge. Even then we were confronted with questions for which there were no ready answers. For instance, by centering on African literature, were we not merely substituting our own for the foreign national tradition? Of course, it makes sense for any country, any nation, to prioritize its literature with the hope that the people would be able to see their own in other literatures and not study it in isolation. We were centering our own and building around it in a certain order Caribbean, African-American, Asian, and Latin American—what's largely taught today as postcolonial—and Euro-American and European. But in reality our "own" was not nation-bound, Africa alone being constituted of many nations and cultures. The language of use alone would have undercut its claim to a self-enclosed nationhood.

Some of these challenges confront the many scholars who have been arguing for the teaching of world literature, or who have already started giving courses on world literature. How, for instance, to se-lect from the vastness? Was it preferable to organize on the model of the great books of civilization on a generic basis—fiction, poetry, drama—or themes, best summed up by David Damrosch when he talks of a paradigm of classics, masterpieces, or simply of windows.[19] Doing justice to world literature, in terms of languages, regions, and periods, is especially difficult when one is thinking of a single course within an otherwise national literature structure. Here, the expan-sion of the postcolonial component would be an adequate beginning. Many departments, even as currently structured, have courses on postcolonial literatures and theories, more so in comparative litera-ture departments. Every department of literature should take cogni-zance of the new synthesis and have it reflected in its organization of literary knowledge.

But I am thinking of a more structural shift: the rise of depart-ments and schools devoted to world literature. Here there would be room for flexibility, experimentation, and exchange of experience, a kind of mixed grill of method and approaches. There are many pos-sibilities, but underlying all is how to balance the national and the global; how to preserve the particularity of a national literature and the intimate relationship between language and literature, while also catering to the global reach and appeal. Gayatri Spivak has noted the virtual exclusion of non-European languages in the Western academy and consistently argued for their inclusion to breathe new life into what would otherwise be death of a discipline in the case of compara-tive literature.[20]

Confronted by the same issues and the vastness of the field, Erich Auerbach, in his article, "Philology and Weltliteratur," talked of the necessity of locating "a point of departure, a handle, as it were, by which the subject can be seized," and then radiate outward.[21] We were not aware of Auerbach at the time, but this was the principle we used at Nairobi. The point of departure can never be prescribed, it will vary from place to place. For us, the point of departure was East Africa, radiating outward to Africa, the Caribbean, and African America, Latin America, Asia, Europe, and the rest. The organizing principle was one of from here to there. Hereness and thereness are mutually contained. It was the same principle we used at the International Center for Writing and Translation at the University of California, Irvine, in organizing our seminars around the twin themes of conversation among languages and other ways of knowing. We started with indigenous American voices and radiated outward to Africa, Asia, and Europe, or a variation of that radiation. Possible variations on the principle are infinite.

Works of imagination are amazingly antinational even where the author may think she or he is espousing national themes. People identify with a good tale and the characters irrespective of the tale's region of origins. Like a mirror or a camera, a work of art may reveal more than consciously intended. Works of imagination refuse to be bound within national geographies; they leap out of nationalist prisons and find welcoming fans outside the geographic walls. But they can also encounter others who want to put them back within the walls, as if they were criminals on the loose.

Equally important, if not more so, are approaches to the text, how we read it. Do we want to welcome it or do we want to put it back into prison—or even a new prison? One can read a literary text with a narrow, short, or wide angle of view. It makes a difference whether one's view is through a concave or convex lens. Reading literature with imperial lenses, for instance, will strongly affect the yield from that literature. Shakespeare can be read as a racial, national, or imperial export or as a mirror of class and national power struggle.

The Siege of Mafeking by the Boers in October 1899 and its relief by the British in May 1900 became a metaphor of intraimperialist war, prefiguring the first and second world wars. Baden-Powell was the hero of Mafeking, the Kiplinglesque Englishman who, with only two thousand officers and men, was able to withstand a 217-day siege by a Boer force of some five thousand men under its commander, Piet Cronje. The relief was greeted as a triumph of the British Empire. Reports of the time describe how the news spread through London, with theater and music hall performances interrupted, crowds swarming into the streets shouting, cheering, dancing, and singing patriotic songs, in a nationwide jingoism with Baden-Powell at its center. Poets of the empire like William Topaz McGonagall wrote of how Baden-Powell and his brave little band had made a bold stand "Against yelling thousands of Boers who were thirsting for their blood." Firm as a rock, he and his band fearlessly stood, even as he kept the people's hearts from breaking from grief "Because he sang to them and did recite / Passages from Shakespeare which did their hearts delight." William Shakespeare had helped the defense of the empire.

Plaatje, a South African black writer who documented the siege in his *Mafeking Diary*, saw it differently. The Anglo-Boer wars (the first, 1880–81; the second, 1899–1902) were fought for the exclusive right of the English or the Dutch to be the sole oppressor of the Africans. Plaatje was a translator of Shakespeare into African languages.

Even as the Siege of Mafeking was taking place, the empire was spreading: the British were colonizing Kenya and opening it to European settlers as another white man's country. Shakespeare became the beloved of the colonial educational establishment; pure art to be liberally dished to schools, but his portrayal of blatant power struggles— with a happy ending in *As You Like*, but a bloody resolution in *Henry IV, Part 2, Macbeth,* and *Julius Caesar*—or the struggle between the feudal and the new bourgeois social order, dramatized in *King Lear*, spoke directly to the struggles for power in Kenya at the time, reflecting accurately the bloody struggle between the Mau Mau guerillas and the forces of the colonial state. Fundamentally, Shakespeare, by extension, questioned the assumed stability of the colonial state, more so than the dreaded *Communist Manifesto* of which many anticolonial nationalists were accused of reading. This was ironic because the *Communist Manifesto* dwells more on the revolutionary character of capitalism than about bloody revolutions against it. Shakespeare dramatized, for all the world to see, that power came from and was maintained by the sword, almost as if he had mastered Machiavelli's conclusion, in his advocacy of force over prayers, that "that all armed prophets have prospered and all unarmed have perished."

The question arises: do we want to free and be freed by the text? It depends on how we read it, and what baggage we bring to it. Hopefully the work of art may contain that which makes us look again, critically, at our baggage. Whether literature is worldly or not may depend on our capacity to release the worldliness in the text. Says Edward Said: "The point is that texts have ways of existing that even in their most rarefied form are always enmeshed in circumstance, time, place, and society—in short, they are in the world, and hence worldly."[22] To release the wordliness in all its multifaceted character, it's perhaps better to read literature, any literature, through a globalectic vision.

Globalectics, derived from the shape of the globe, is the mutual containment of hereness and thereness in time and space, where time and space are also in each other. It's the Blakean vision of a world in a grain of sand and eternity in an hour.

Reading globaletically is a way of approaching any text from whatever times and places to allow its content and themes form a free conversation with other texts of one's time and place, the better to make it yield its maximum to the human. It is to allow it to speak to our own cultural present even as we speak to it from our own cultural present. It is to read a text with the eyes of the world; it is to see the world with the eyes of the text.

Such reading should bring into mutual impact and comprehension the local and the global, the here and there, the national and the world. Even old classical literatures of different cultures and languages can be read globaletically.

One of the obstacles to a globalectic reading is the tendency to look at literature and the languages of its birth in terms of hierarchy, the notion that some languages and cultures are inherently of a higher order than others. This is the current relationship between languages, what elsewhere I have called linguistic feudalism, with an aristocracy of languages at the top and menial barbaric languages at the bottom. In this hierarchical view, a few European languages—principally English, French, Russian, German, Italian, and Spanish—are the aristocracy, and those from Asia, Africa, Latin America, indigenous America, and the rest are ranged in a descending order of power and prestige. Literature and culture tend to be valued according to what position their language of composition occupies in the hierarchy. This leads to aesthetic feudalism within and between nations. And it is fatal to any attempts to organize literature on a world basis, no matter the selected point of departure. I like the sound of Auerbach when he says that "our philological home is the earth; it can no longer be the nation."[23] This attitude is germane to a global consciousness of our common humanity. World literature, of which the postcolonial is an integral part, is our common heritage as much as the air webreathe.

I have argued for a collapsing of this hierarchy so as to view the relationship between languages, cultures, and literatures in terms of a network, akin but not identical to Deleuze and Guattari's "rhizome." In a network there is no one center, all are points balanced and related to one another by the principle of giving and receiving. The pedagogical organization of literature should reflect that sense of a common heritage of simultaneously taking and giving assumed by a network.

Central to the pedagogical enterprise is the practice of translation. Translation is the language of languages. It opens the gates of national and linguistic prisons. It is thus one of the most important allies of world literature and global consciousness. But most important is the globalectic reading of the word. Globaletics becomes the way of reading world literature. Globalectical reading means breaking open the prison house of imagination built by theories and outlooks that would seem to signify the content within is classified, open to only a few. This involves declassifying theory in the sense of making it accessible—a tool for clarifying interactive connections and interconnections of social phenomena and their mutual impact in the local and global space, a means of illuminating the internal and the external, the local and the global dynamics of social being. This may also mean the act of reading becoming also a process of self-examination.

However, concealed within each language is another hierarchical schema that stands as a barrier to globalectical imagination: that of the written "versus" the oral, literature against orature. The politics and pedagogy that have surrounded that schema is the subject of my final chapter.

THE ORAL NATIVE AND
THE WRITING MASTER
Orature, Orality, and Cyborality

4 Aesthetic feudalism, arising from placing cultures in a hierarchy, is best seen in the relationship between oral and written languages, where the oral, even when viewed as being "more" authentic or closer to the natural, is treated as the bondsman to the writing master. With orality taken as the source for the written and orature as the raw material for literature, both were certainly placed on a lower rung in the ladder of achievement and civilization.

It has not always been the case that orality or speech was regarded with less esteem than the written, the basis for expelling some cultures from history and complex thoughts, consigning them to a place in hell. In Plato's *Phaedrus*, speech is seen as the living and animate, the proper residence for the science of the dialectic, as opposed to the written which "trundles about everywhere in the same way"—a phantom.[1] And for Aristotle, words spoken were signs of the soul while words written were merely signs of words spoken.[2] There is of course the subversive irony against Socrates' claims on behalf of speech in that his dialogues, including the argument between him and Phaedrus, have continually remained animate through the ages because

This essay expands considerably the arguments in my paper, "Notes towards a Performance Theory of Orature," *Performance Research* 12, no. 3 (Fall 2007): 4–7. See also Ngũgĩ wa Thiong'o, "Oral Power and Europhone Glory: Orature, Literature, and Stolen Legacies," in *Penpoints, Gunpoints, and Dreams: Toward a Critical Theory of the Arts and the State in Africa* (Oxford: Clarendon Press, 1998).

of writing. The two interlocutors are not, of course, in a position to know that writing would make possible the afterlife of their exchange, including Socrates' argument for the oral against the letter.

Even in the European Middle Ages, and wherever there were forms of writing, the written and oral performance (singing, reading aloud, playing, etc.) were genuinely coexistent and interactive as "equals."

The hegemony of the written over the oral comes with the printing press, the dominance of capitalism, and colonization. This hegemony, or its perception, has roots in the rider-and-the-horse pairing of master and slave, or colonizer and colonized, a process in which the latter begins to be demonized as the possessor of deficiencies, including of languages.[3] The absence of a writing system—ideographic, hieroglyphic, or, mostly, alphabetic—is taken as the prime evidence. What we witness in this context is a double colonization: first, a language is seen as lower than another in general, and second, its oral ontology is considered to be lower than the written "being" of the dominant other.

Let's take the examples of Karen Blixen (Isak Dinesen) and Claude Lévi-Strauss, a choice partly motivated by the fact that they are good evocative writers, able to tell a story and create scene and character, as in their books *Out of Africa* (1937) and *Tristes Tropiques* (1955), but mainly because they are not directly members of the ruling authority over the peoples about whom they write, respectively the Agīkūyū of Kenya and the Nambikwara of Brazil. Eighteen years lie between the two publications, but the writing scene between Dinesen and Jogona (Njūgūna) of Kenya and the writing lesson between Lévi-Strauss and the Nambikwara chief of Brazil are strikingly similar in their colonial attitudes toward the oral.

Blixen was a Danish settler in an English colony and probably had a different view of the natives than the English; Lévi-Strauss was a French anthropologist and probably viewed the natives of the Brazilian jungle differently than the ruling Portuguese-speaking authorities. Both establish an empathy with "their" respective natives, which may have given the authors the illusion of knowing the native mind and therefore self-confidence in interpreting for the benefit of their reading audience in Europe what they see as strange and infantile in the behavior of their natives. This may account for such felicitous categorical conclusions as Blixen's that natives do not fear death and know nothing of gratitude[4] or Lévi-Strauss's that the Nambikwara were unable to draw except for a few dots and zigzags on their calabashes. Both Blixen and Lévi-Strauss look at the oral through the eyes of the written. Both claim to have introduced writing to the native community: Blixen by establishing a farm school, Lévi-Strauss by the comical act of literally throwing paper and pencils on the ground as a gift, more or less gesturing: there is my gift of writing. Lévi-Strauss did not, of course, intend it to be seen as comical.

The gift's recipient, the chief of the Nambikwara, makes horizontal lines on the paper and then puts on a show of reading from them as the basis of distributing the rest of the gifts, in the way he had seen the anthropologist consult his notes. Lévi-Strauss, who participates in the make-believe, concludes that the chief, in going through the motions of literacy to "astonish his companions . . . convince them that he was in alliance with the whiteman and shared his secrets," has grasped that writing, regardless of whether or not he can read, is power.[5] "Writing, on that occasion, had made its appearance, among the Nambikwara," Lévi-Strauss says, as he reflects on the exchange of the gifts later that night.[6] He may think of writing as a dangerous thing, since it brings in social stratification and exploitation—better the innocence of an oral culture—but Lévi-Strauss still sees writing as a marker of a boundary between the savage Nambikwara chief and the civilized Lévi-Strauss, possessor of writing. Derrida, in *Of Grammatology*, criticizes Lévi-Strauss's assertion that "the Nambikwara had no written language before," asking how far it was legitimate not to call by the name of writing those few dots and zigzags on their calabashes. It is not necessary to extend the term *writing* to every signifying system, as Derrida does to the Nambikwara's, for the issue is not the name given to different signifying systems but their hierarchical relations of power.

In fact, despite his assertions, Lévi-Strauss plays along, takes the lines and the zigzags the chief is making as writing, and even pretends to be able to read and understand them, the way one might do to a child holding a pen and making similar marks. The anthropologist thinks that he is toying with the mind of the chief and in alliance with him duping the people, as a result of what he describes as "an unspoken agreement between us that his scribblings had a meaning that I pretended to decipher." But among the three parties, who is playing with whom? The chief is probably the most highly cultured person in his community, who knows the nuances of the words and thought of his own language. His judgment and oratory, and his knowledge of the history, philosophy, and the environment of his community, are probably unsurpassed, for this was what would have propelled him to the position of chief in the first place. Whatever the marks he puts on paper, it cannot surely be for the sole purpose of impressing his people with his knowledge, for they know, and he knows they know, that he cannot write and read any more than they can. In the same vein, he must know that his guest knows that he cannot read and write. Reading the same lesson, its open air staging, its arbitrary abruptness, its spatial arrangement of giver and recipients, Gabriele Schwab sees the reaction of the chief not as infantile behavior in imitation of the adult but as a tongue-in-cheek performance of relations of power at the expense of Lévi-Strauss. "The chief mimes the practice of writing as an instrument of power while at the same time using that very power against the anthropologist, thus subverting the latter's claim to superiority."[7] It is a performance, the forest as the stage, the two lead actors, the oral native and the writing master, dueling it out in front of a captive audience bounded by trees, bush and foliage, their faces lit by fire or moonlight. One can imagine that the play of shadows and light deepens the gravitas of the occasion. If the chief were in a position to describe the same encounter, he would tell a very different version of the event. At the very least he would not describe it as a writing lesson, nor would he confuse the gift of paper and pen with the gift of writing and therefore conclude that writing had come to his people.

The writing lesson is reminiscent of the education scene between Crusoe and Friday. Lévi-Strauss is clearly aware of Defoe's text, for one of the chapters that follows the writing lesson is titled "Robinson Crusoe." Extending Schwab's kind of reading, Friday may also be letting Crusoe, the teaching master, prolong the assumption that the man is without a name. Friday knows that he has another name, given to him at birth. Both play with each other, Crusoe by withholding his real name of Robinson in order to establish a colonial hierarchy of master and servant, and Friday by withholding his proper name while pretending to play the colonizer's game of the naming master and the named native. Friday comes from cultures where a person may have multiple given names, in addition to the real proper name, like having a protective layer on what is precious. Crusoe may thereafter continue thinking that he knows the native, but the one thing that the native is sure of is that the master does not know his name. For the master, this may produce the self-illusion of the quiescent native, but the native's sure knowledge that the master does not really know him may be the seed of a more critical and ultimately rebellious consciousness.

The performance of Lévi-Strauss and the Nambikwara chief, the writing master and the oral native, mirrors that of Blixen and Jogona, only that one takes place in the rainy forests of the Amazon and the other in the temperate climate of the Ngong Hills area, not far from Nairobi, the capital. Lévi-Strauss studies the "savage" mind to understand the nature of human "civilized society" where Blixen studies wildlife to give her an understanding of the native mind. I am not sure what's more astonishing in Blixen's *Out of Africa*: her claim that the aptitude to stillness she had learned from the behavior of the wild animals of the country was later useful to her in her dealings with native people, or her playing God to the same natives through the magic art of writing à la fictional Prospero. The episode occurs in a lengthy chapter, "A Shooting Accident on the Farm," in which Wamai, son of Jogona (Njũgũna), one of her farm workers, is shot dead by another child with a gun left loaded by Belknap, one of Blixen's white managers. There is not a hint of Belknap having done wrong or being held responsible for what happens. The children were playing "whiteman" with the gun. When Jogona is later awarded forty-five goats from the father of the boy who "caused" the accident, four other men turn up to claim their share on the basis of their biological kinship to a boy they had never raised. Jogona is not Wamai's biological father and for them biology trumps social fact. It is this quandary that prompts Jogona to approach Blixen one morning and ask her to "write for him the account of his relations to the dead child and its family,"[8] a document he would take to the colonial district commissioner of the area in support of his legitimate claims. Jogona transmits the words orally; Blixen, the scribe, gives them visual marks on paper, and then reads the tale back to him.

Blixen describes how, as she reads out his name, Jogona swiftly turns his face to her and gives her "a great fierce flaming glance, so exuberant with laughter that it changed the old man into a boy, into the very symbol of youth," a glance he repeats, "this time deepened and calmed, with a new dignity,"[9] after she reads his name again where it figures as verification below his thumb mark. The mark signifies his authorship of the tale. By writing his name below the thumb mark, Blixen, the scribe, is helping indicate that the thumbprint is Jogona's. But the transcribed words, if faithfully rendered, are Jogona's, his oral signature, his presence, to use the Derridian terms. Presumably Jogona is grateful for the scribe's faithful rendering of his tale and oral signature. But mainly he is proud of his authorship of the tale. In reality both the oral and the written, though the latter is via a scribe, work together to confirm that authorship and ownership. But the scribe sees the whole thing differently. The written trumps the oral and the writing master, the oral native. She has created him, given him proof of his existence, and his glance of gratitude is to her as his creator: "Such a glance did Adam give the Lord when He formed him out of the dust, and breathed into his nostrils the breath of life, and man became a living soul. I had created him and shown him himself: Jogona Kanyagga of life everlasting."[10]

This passage has echoes of Shakespeare's eighteenth sonnet:

So long as men can breathe, or eyes can see,
So long lives this, and this gives life to thee.

But in Blixen's case it is spoken condescendingly from godly heights, and the echoes are more of Prospero and Caliban. Prior to their contact, Caliban had no means of knowing himself, according to Prospero:

. . . When thou didst not, savage,
Know thine own meaning, but wouldst gabble like
A thing most brutish, I endow'd thy purposes
With words that made them known.[11]

Blixen is of course not scolding Jogona, but her claims of endowing his purposes with written words are similar in intent. She follows this claim with a discourse on writing and then a description of a comedy, probably not intended, in which Jogona for days after, would waylay her everywhere, so that she might read the tale again. She indulges him, as one might a child who demands the same story over and over again, and "at each reading his face took on the same impress of religious triumph."[12]

Blixen's perspective is clearly consistent with the colonial view that prehistory and history were congruent with the oral and the written. She captures this in her summary of the entire writing and reading saga; it was as if Jogona had suddenly jumped from the vagueness of the oral into the clarity of history. It was Plato's elixir of memory. The past that had been so elusive, "and changing every time it was thought of, had here been caught, conquered, and pinned down before his very eyes. It had become history."[13] The Danish knight in literary armor, she is a landed baroness after all, gets off her horse and wrestles down the elusive dragon of time that had plagued the native. The document, it must be pointed out, does help Jogona sustain his claims, but in Blixen's vision, it has done more than that: writing has brought Jogona from the darkness of prehistory to the light of history. Even though Jogona cannot read what's written for him about him, just like the many chiefs who had been made to sign away their lands and destinies by putting a thumb mark on documents drawn and written for them by their adversaries, the written document was now proof of Jogona's existence, as it had become proof of the legal validity of treaties and contracts between the colonizer and the colonized. To Blixen, it is not the recall of his successful legal claims that brings Jogona instant pleasure and pride. It is not even his words as such but the words as given visibility by her writing grace. The aesthetic takes center stage.

The oral aesthetic has been buried under the weight of the written, just as the validity of the oral in colonial life had been supplanted by that of the written, whether as evidence in law disputes or sources in historical research.

Blixen's claim that it is writing that has transformed Jogona's prehistoric past into history is part of a general theme in the colonial conception of what constituted history and historical evidence. Although oral sources in the writing of history had always been used by historians as far back as Herodotus, they became suspect when in the 1950s African scholars started claiming their use as part of the research methodology in African history. It took the fighting pioneering spirit of those African historians—led principally by Bethwell Allan Ogot of Kenya and Kenneth Onwuka Dike of Nigeria—to have oral sources accepted as valid by universities and institutions of higher learning in Africa and the world. Drawing from oral and written sources, they produced groundbreaking works in African historiography, Ogot with his *History of the Southern Luo: Volume I, Migrations and Settlement, 1500–1900* and Dike with his *Trade and Politics in the Niger Delta, 1830–55: An Introduction to the Economic and Political History of Nigeria*. Though the heavy lifting was done by African scholars, others like Jan Vansina added their voices, and now, orality, as an integral part of valid sources in historical research, is universally accepted in the academy.[14] By 1979, when Allan Ogot became president of the International Scientific Committee for the drafting of the general history of Africa, he could write, not without satisfaction, that the UNESCO-sponsored history would be based on a "wide variety of sources, including oral tradition and art forms."[15] Since then, the UNESCO project has blossomed into eight scholarly volumes on African history, translated into several languages and popularized by the same number of abridged paperback volumes.

It is an interesting historical irony, but one that carries parallels and signals continuity, that Allan Ogot, a pioneer in many other cultural initiatives in the postindependence era, happened to be the dean of the Faculty of Arts of the University of Nairobi in 1968 when the debate over the organization of literary studies broke out, in particular over the place and role of oral literature in a new dispensation. It must have amused him to see the three literary musketeers, Henry Owuor Anyumba, Taban lo Liyong, and me, fighting battles he had already fought as if they were new. They may have been old news in history, but in a literature dominated by English studies, they were new and we fought with the energy and fervor of a new discovery from our headquarters, a nondescript café on Koinange Street.

We were an incongruous threesome, each a graduate of English: Taban lo Liyong had studied at Washington University and the Iowa Writers' Workshop; Anyumba had studied at Makerere University and Caius College, Cambridge; and I had studied at Makerere University and Leeds University. I was a member of the English Department, the only Kenyan and African at the time, and Anyumba and Liyong were research fellows in the Cultural Division of the Institute of Development Studies. Both were researching oral literature.[16] Taban was essentially a writer who, before he left the United States, had gone so far as to declare East Africa a literary desert. Now he was helping in greening it through his own work and his discovery of a rich oral tradition among the Maasai. For Anyumba, this had always been his passion, and at Makerere where he had graduated with a two-year diploma in education in 1956, he was the recipient of a research prize for his essay, "The Place of Folk Tales in the Education of Luo Children." Even as a teacher at Friend's School, Kamusinga, from 1957 through 1963, he was often seen in the field with a camera,[17] recorder, and notebooks, interacting with musicians, dancers, and performers and showing fascination for their musical instruments. He was admitted to Caius College, Cambridge, in 1963 and by the time he graduated three years later he had published papers on Luo poetry in the Nigerian journal *Black Orpheus*, founded and edited by Ulli Beier. Along the way he had earned an international reputation as a musicologist among his peers. The otherwise self-effacing Anyumba was a passionate advocate of the oral and he could not imagine a reorganized literary space, much less join it, if it did not include oral literature.

In the call for reorganization, it was noted that while Africa was littered with oral literature, this plenitude was invisible in literature departments. The arts communicated orally and received aurally were seen as belonging on a lower rung in the linear development of literature. Oral literature, as an integral part of a reorganized department, would help forge a new literary dispensation, which, by discovering and proclaiming loyalty to indigenous values, "would on the one hand be set in the stream of history to which it belongs and so be better appreciated; and on the other be better able to embrace and assimilate other thoughts without losing its roots."[18]

Anyumba was not one to sing his own praises, but he must have had a sense of satisfaction to see the area to which he had devoted his life as a student, teacher, and researcher finally find a respectable place in the newly renamed Department of Literature and later in the English Department at Makerere University in Uganda, where oral literature shared equal billing in the curriculum with written literature from Africa and throughout the world.

But debates over the term and the concept of oral literature continued in the corridors of departments and in conferences. It was an oxymoron. The problem lay in the English language. In Gĩkũyũ, *Kĩrĩra*, the term for literature, is inclusive of the written and the oral. One can talk of *Kĩrĩra gĩa Kanua* (oral literature) or *Kĩrĩra gĩa Karamu* (written literature) when clarification is necessary. *Fasihi* in Kiswahili functions the same way: *Fasihi-simulizi* denotes oral and *Fasihi-andishi* denotes written, both equally *Fasihi*. In Gĩkũyũ and Kiswahili, the terms do not carry "the preconceived ranking of art forms."[19]

Pio Zirimu, the Ugandan linguist then on the faculty of the Department of English at Makerere, coined the term *orature* as an alternative to the oxymoron but also as a counter to the assumed inferiority of the oral to the literary arts. Orature was to orality what literature was to writing. Zirimu rejected the equation between orality and illiteracy, for the latter, coming out of the binary opposition of literate and illiterate, posited the literate as the norm and relegated the illiterate to an offshoot. But why make one the norm and the other the departure from the norm? The real binary was "orate" and "literate" and they were not oppositional absolutes; they were connected by the word; they had their adequacies and inadequacies as representations of thought and experience. Writing and orality were natural allies, not antagonists; so also orature and literature.

Zirimu never lived long enough to develop the concept extensively; his life was untimely cut short by the brutal Idi Amin dictatorship, whose agents poisoned him in Nigeria during the famous Festac '77. But his brief definition of orature as the use of utterance as an aesthetic means of expression remains tantalizing, pointing to an oral system of aesthetics that did not need validity from the literary, the implied need of such validity being a product of the literary colonization of orality.

The term lived on after his departure. It has spread, and today one reads variously of Hawaiian Orature, Namibian Orature, Ghanaian Orature, and many others. However, it is still not yet used universally and the struggle between it and the oxymoron as the name for the oral aesthetic still continues.[20] Most use the term and the oxymoron interchangeably. Its usage is nonetheless increasing as more and more scholars engage with the term and tease out the various theoretical possibilities inherent in the elements and features that constitute the oral aesthetic and reason.[21]

The feature that most intrigues students of the oral aesthetic is what in the abolition statement we had described as the "interlinked nature of art forms in the traditional practice." Verbal forms, in other words, were not always distinct from dance and music. Within music, we argued, there was close correspondence between verbal and melodic tones; within metrical lyrics, the poetic text was inseparable from the tune; and the folktale often bore an operatic form with sung refrain as an integral part. The distinction between prose and poetry was absent or very fluid. The oral aesthetic also has social functions, arising from its intimate relationship and involvement with society. Its study was therefore seen as leading to a multidisciplinary outlook with links to literature, music, linguistics, sociology, anthropology, history, psychology, religion, and philosophy. Drawing from the "spontaneity and liberty of communication inherent in oral transmission—openness to sounds, sights, rhythms, tones, in life and the environment"—could lead to a mindset "characterized by the willingness to experiment with new form," in short, a willingness to connect.[22]

The interlinkage of art forms is best described in J. P. Clark–Bekederemo's introduction to the Ijaw epic, *Ozidi*. The saga was told and acted in seven nights. Clark-Bekederemo recorded it in audio and on film, translated it into English, and then had the English, side by side with the Ijaw, published by Ibadan University Press in 1977. Clark-Bekederemo is a leading Nigerian poet, playwright, and essayist. He has published essays titled *The Example of Shakespeare*, but after working for many years on the *Ozidi*, he has given us a great example of orature. But since, as in all cases of attempting to write down classical epics, what is captured in writing is a particular version, a particular rendering among many possible oral narrations, Clark-Bekederemo insists that his *The Ozidi Saga* is a literary rendering of the version performed by Okabou Ojobolo. Even so, what Clark-Bekederemo says of the artistry of the saga, its deployment of the multiple media of words, music, dance, drama, and ritual can be taken to characterize the oral aesthetic in general.

According to Clark-Bekederemo, the saga was more than a verbal composition. It was "a composite art, a multi-faceted piece whose other integral parts" were "the visual, representing the dramatic character of the work; the ritual representing its religious significance" and then the auditory side, "the music, vocal as well as instrumental, impregnating the work from beginning to the end." It was the interlinkage of all those attributes, not any one of them, that gave *The Ozidi Saga* "its totality of being,"[23] and he wondered whether the term *oral literature* was adequate, musing that Wagnerian opera was nearer the mark.

Interlinkage is at the heart of the theories that have attempted to take the term *orature* beyond its Zirimian usage. Pitika Ntuli, the South African sculptor and poet, is a pertinent example. He is now back home in South Africa. But in his years of exile in 1980s London, working with the multinational, multicontinental performance group African Dawn, he reacted strongly to what he saw as the atomization of life and culture in Western bourgeois society and recognized in the oral-aural arts of the African people a healing opposite, a wholeness. In the arts of his childhood, he saw no boundaries between art forms. Instead, what he experienced was fluidity between drama, story, song, discourse, and performance. In "Orature: A Self-Portrait," Pitika claims that a fusion of all art forms was the basic characteristic of orature. But it was more than that, it was kind of *Gestalt*, the wholeness being bigger than the parts that contributed to it. He put it more poetically: "Orature is more than the fusion of all art forms. It is the conception and reality of a total view of life. It is the capsule of feeling, thinking, imagination, taste and hearing. It is the flow of a creative spirit."[24] He expressed the interconnectedness of phenomena in terms of a "beginning come full circle on a higher plane."[25] Like Pio Zirimu before him, Pitika Ntuli has not elaborated on this essay, though he may yet do so, but it remains among the most intriguing treatments of the concept, particularly its central core of fusion and connections that made up the wholeness.

Micere Mugo best captures orature's aesthetic reflection of the interconnectedness of reality, what she describes as layers and layers of interrelated coexistence, in her onion structure theory, which, she writes, begins with a nucleus, or inner core, at the center of its being. "The shape of this nucleus/core is round or circular. This is then surrounded by accumulating layers . . . layers upon layers of increasing solidity. The layers also become larger and larger, or wider and wider in their 'circularness' as we move outwards—away from the core/nucleus. These embracing and connecting circles or rings maintain tight contact with each other, harmoniously making one whole." Orature reflects a reality of connected circles from the inner being of the individual and social person to the outmost circle of "the sun, the moon, the stars, the sky and the rest of the elements."[26]

He does not call it orature, but Kamau Brathwaite's description of the properties of what he terms the magical realism within folktext captures the same web of interconnections: "enjambements of time/place/consciousness w/in continuums of these; the capacity of all created things to 'become' (bom-bam) one another—humanification of birds, plants, animals, minerals & vice versa—anthropomorphing, animamorphing, oral/echo, mur-alization—ultimately, for some, the carnivalization don't like how this sounds—of experience."[27]

The dynamic inter-linkage of art forms in orature is thus seen as reflecting a *Weltanschauung* that assumes the normality of the connection between nature, nurture, supernatural, and supernurtural. I have written on all this in *Penpoints, Gunpoints, and Dreams*, but it is necessary to elaborate further here. Each of these realms is a particular expression of the primary substance that connects them. In the Gīkūyū system of thought detectable in the language, this substratum (substance) is *ndū (du)*. Mū*ndū* stands for human; Kī*ndū* for a thing; ha*ndū* and kū*ndū* for place and space; ū*ndū* for phenomenon; and hī*ndī* for time or, more appropriately, space-time. Ū*mūndū* (utu in Kiswahili) stands for the quality of being human. *Ndū (du)* is the *ntu* in all Bantu languages. It would seem to stand for that which connects material and abstract being, the being of phenomenal nature, nurture, thought, and spirit. In my novel *Wizard of the Crow*, one of the characters, called AG, goes around the fictional territory of Aburīria looking for this *ndū* he thinks is the key to understanding the secret of all life. *Ndū* is the primary substance of all being: it expresses the interdependence of all existence, physical and abstract, that people must have detected in the reality surrounding their lives.

Humans are definitely of nature. In that sense they are not different from animals and plants that all depend on the same mother-environment of earth, air, water, and sun. Orature assumes this. Hence in the narratives of orature, humans, birds, animals, and plants interact freely, often change into each others' forms, and share language. Humans in distress talk to birds and give them messages to deliver. In a Gīkūyū tale of the ogre, the blacksmith, and a pregnant woman, it's Bird, after being fed with castor-oil seeds, who takes a message to the smith, working far away, about the ogre who threatens the smith's wife and children, like the biblical dove sent by Noah to survey the land after the flood. The Homeric epics *The Iliad* and *The Odyssey* assume the same interactive mutuality between the various realms of being, the gods at times entering the battlefield in support of their different favorite combatants. Clearest on this is Ovid's *Metamorphoses* where different forms of being change into each other—change itself being the central theme, as he says at the opening: "I want to speak about bodies that changed into new forms." Similarly the Indian epics Mahabharata and Ramayana and Hindu mythology in general embody change: Vishnu, the third of the Hindu triad that includes Brahma and Shiva, has nine reincarnations, some into animal forms.

Nature in orature manifests itself as a web of connections of mutual dependence, the Pitikian full circle or Mugo's onion structure of being. This web of connections reflects the language of nature; the various aspects of nature are in active communications within themselves, for instance, in each biological unit between and within cells. But they are also in active communication with other entities, for instance the rain circle of water, vapor, clouds, rain, rivers, lakes, and seas, the subject of poetry and song. It is seen in the interaction between bees and butterflies with flowers, a process that enables fertilization between plants. Eliminate all bees and butterflies, and famine descends to threaten human life. Everywhere one looks in nature is a web of connections, even among the seemingly unconnected.

Nurture, in general, mimics the structures and communications of nature. The entire human transportation system including rockets and space ships are an extension of the leg; the entire machine-making technology, the hand; the telescopic system, the eye; the telecommunication systems, the ear; and the latest, computer technology and cyberspace, the brain. Nurture comes out of nature. Just as nature has given rise to nurture, nurture itself has given rise to cyberture, the virtual reality that has become part of our lives. Cyberture is to nurture what nurture is to nature. It mimics nurture in the same way that nurture mimics nature. This does not mean that these realms, particularly the new technologies, are always acting in harmony. Activities in the realm of nurture, for instance the unregulated emission of gases that contribute to global warming, can seriously disrupt the rhythms of nature, and those of cyberture, for instance the ease of communications that enables global finance capital to move in and out of countries, can disrupt those of nurture and nature. But this is a result of organization and the uses to which such gains are put, to enhance or disrupt the wealth of human spirituality.

The major generic elements of classical orature—riddle, proverb, story, song, poetry, drama, dance, and myth—like the other aesthetic products of the imagination, the pictorial and the sculptural for instance, have also simultaneously nourished the imagination and explained the universe, helping humans to come to terms with it. The arts are to the imagination what food is to the body and spirituality to the soul, but they have the added character of guiding all human activities. That's why the arts in general, orature in particular, have always been part of human society.

The riddle as an image reflects the riddle of a universe, with its contradictory core of a unity around which coheres many forms of being, which is one in many. It seeks resemblances and parallels, among the apparently diverse and contradictory. Naturally, the riddle litters narratives of many cultures, as it does those of ancient Greece. For instance, in Sophocles, Oedipus gives a correct answer to a riddle, which has otherwise baffled the whole population, but the answer sets him on the tragic journey to glorious heights and inglorious depths. Odysseus's journey from Troy back to Ithaca involves facing many riddles. Riddling is frequently an integral part of the challenges of an evening entertainment. This often takes the form of challenges to the memory and knowledge, since many of the riddles and their answers are already known. But there are other challenges that involve creation of new riddles. Inventing a new riddle and its solution, as opposed to the recitation of old ones, involves observation and leaps of imagination to connect the apparently unconnected. The Agĩkũyũ Gĩcandĩ performance involves two or three champions of improvisation, wit, and observation, competing with each other in public, trying to tie each other in knots in a series of riddles. Since the audience does not know any of the riddles in advance, they are the judges because the riddle and the solution have to be aesthetically satisfying, instantaneously. Many of these become part of the communal repertoire, and are passed on from generation to generation, to become communal lore. In the Agĩkũyũ riddles, *I have a house without a door*, whose answer is egg, or *I have a companion who never tells me rest*, whose solution is road or shadow, are examples of the many riddles that children learn and use to compete with each other in the evenings. But the real inventions come from the competing champions, although even children may try to create their own. And even then, what the children create is also judged by the same criteria: it has to be aesthetically satisfying. Otherwise the teller of an unsatisfactory riddle is greeted, with no, no, it's not true—an interesting response, since the surface of a riddle is not factually true. But the notion of a good and a bad, or a true and an untrue, riddle remains, because the heart of a riddle has to beat a truth. The riddle can often be part of a story.

The proverb, famously described in Achebe's *Things Fall Apart* as the palm oil with which words are eaten among the Ibo, is important in all cultures. A proverb, a codification of wisdom, has the three parts of the cognitive process: a sensory experience from which emerges a story that in turn becomes the basis of a universal, generalizing pithy statement applicable in similar situations. The proverb codes the moral of the story, itself obviously drawn from observations of characteristic behavior of humans and animals. Dr. Wanjohi's book *The Wisdom and Philosophy of the Gikuyu Proverbs*, in which he discusses metaphysics, epistemology, and ethics, is based on the study of the proverb entirely.

The story is all-pervasive in orature. It has its basis in the human confrontation with time. Nobody knows what will happen in the next hour, day, week, month, year, or years to come—in short, the future. The biggest unknown is what happens after death. In a story, as opposed to real life, one can know what happens next. Indeed, the central element of a story is the question of what happens next, a question also central in visual narratives and actions like sports. In a sports event, say tennis, soccer, baseball, or football, as much as in a story, what happens next, an unknown future, becomes known. That's why in the world of Anansi, the question of the ownership of the story is central in the struggle between Anansi and other animals. The owner of the story is the conqueror of time. She or he is a prophet. In all cases, a story and the storyteller raise an anxiety of expectation satisfied only by the final denouement. A good storyteller is the one who raises anew the anxiety of expectation that he then goes on to satisfy. Even when listeners already know the general outline of a story and its ending, the master storyteller is still able to recreate afresh the anxiety of expectation and then satisfy it. The story becomes new in every telling and retelling. It embraces all the other elements of orature, especially the song, which punctuates the narrative as a chorus in which even the listeners can join. Myth and legend are part of the story genre and stand somewhere between fiction, history, and religion. The owners of the Yoruba, Hindu, Greek, Egyptian, Hebrew, or any other pantheon may not see the deities as pure fiction: they are rooted in those culture's history and world outlook. The celebration of this pantheon involves all the other elements including song, dance, and the story again.

More all-pervasive than story is song. Song is there in all struggles with nature (hunting songs, work songs) and nurture (war songs and work songs); physical and psychic health (songs that heal and entertain the body); and in spirituality (songs that accompany religious rites). In the beginning, according to St. John, was the word, which then became flesh and thus launched creation, but since sound preceded the word, for the word is a particular organization of sound, we can say with Sikhism and Hinduism that in the beginning was the sound *om*. Then, we may add, came song, word, and then language. At any rate, song and word are conjoined in sound. Sound organized as music commands the body and mind. The body responds to the sound of music in form of motion, body motion, or what goes by the name of dance. In Gĩkũyũ, *Rwĩmbo*, the word for song, also indicates dance and ceremony, as an equivalent word did among Mesoamericans when the Spanish invaded their lands.

Dance is a celebration of freedom from fixity, a momentary triumph over gravitational pull, a symbolic conquest of gravity. Some balletic moves are spectacular and breathtaking, when the dancer literally seems to fly. Maasai dancers, body upright, hands held straight and tightly by the body, launch themselves in the air from a standing position. Dance is often accompanied by song and, combined, the two are a celebration of sound and motion. Motion is inherent in change, growth, and development in nature and nurture. Life is motion, for we know that a thing is dead when it ceases to move.

The key in all these elements of orature is their interpenetration as pointed out by Anyumba, Clark-Bedekereme, Pitika Ntuli, Micere Mugo, and others. But central to them is performance. Each of the elements—story, riddle, song, and so on—constitutes a performance genre. Performance is the central feature of orature, or as Kĩmani Njogu and Rocha Chimerah have put it, *Utendaji ni uti wa mgongo wa fasihi simulizi*,[28] and this differentiates the concept from that of literature and makes the oxymoron all the more gravely distorting.

Performance involves the performer and audience, and in orature, the performer and audience interact. Anywhere from the fireside, village square, and market place to the shrine can serve as the performance space and mise-en-scène. The carnival takes place in the streets, wherever there seems an open space, and means mass participation. Whatever the combination of location, time, and audience, orature realizes its fullness in performance. There's no metaphysics of absence in performance, only that of presence, except of course when the performance, as in Clark-Bekederemo's *Ozidi Saga*, is recorded in audio, written, and other visual forms. In such a case, as in *Phaedrus*, the written makes possible the continued resurrection of absence into a presence.

Orature is not pure metaphysics or a zombie that comes alive only when inhabiting the body of the written and other recorded forms. It is a dynamic living presence in all cultures. In the case of Africa, the authors of the "On the Abolition of the English Department" stressed the fact that "the art did not end yesterday; it is a living tradition," it is a presence in religious functions, births, funerals, marriages, nightlife, and politics. In the anticolonial resistance, song and dance played a pivotal role in recruiting, rallying, and coding the social vision. The colonial authorities feared orature more than they did literature. A good example is Kenya, where the authorities continually banned music and dance, often imprisoning defiant participants. When in 1921 the colonial state imprisoned Harry Thuku, the workers' leader of the day, and also killed 150 protesting workers outside the Norfolk Hotel in Nairobi, the women invented a new song and dance, Kanyegenyūri, that kept alive Harry Thuku's name. The dance and the words were erotic but lethal as a rallying call expressing their hope to give birth to more heroes with the absent Harry Thuku as their collective lover.

> After they took Harry Thuku
> I felt this great desire
> Titillating my groins
> I want to sing and dance
> I am looking for a partner
> So I can give birth to victory

If Harry Thuku was my lover
I'd hide him between my thighs
Always with me in the fields
And as I go for firewood
Or pound millet at home.

The colonial state banned the dance. But the women continued, defiantly, leading to arrests and harassments. They responded to this with more defiance in words and dance:

For the Kanyegenyūri (dance)
Rebels took an oath
To always dance it
But the colonialist said
It's illegal
Look at me now
We are still dancing it.
Black people are fearless
Their children are fearless
Their patriots are fearless
Should I live in fear
Who would I take after?

There were others like the Muthirigu dance of the 1940s, sung and danced by young men who once again defied threats of prisons and death:

They say the dance's banned
Comrade dancer
Did you read the letter banning it?
You threaten us with prisons
You threaten us with prisons
Your handcuffs are decorative bangles
Dance fearlessly
Ye native people
The way we'll dance

And turn to dust
The floor of Kamĩtĩ Prison.[29]

The climax came in the 1950s when the colonial state banned all songs and dances associated with Mau Mau and the militant politics of the anticolonial resistance. But in the mountains and forests, the Mau Mau guerrilla fighters continued coding in song and dance their gains and losses in different battles. Most of the melodies have endured and they are still as fresh and moving as when they were composed under such harsh conditions. This is true of other situations all over Africa, from the Angolan struggles against Portuguese rule to Zimbabwe and South Africa against white minority rule. The case of the Caribbean and Afro-America is even more telling: from the freedom spirituals (negro spirituals) to hip hop, Afro-Caribbean and African-American orature has played a central role in the molding of modern culture in the Caribbean and America and its impact has been felt in global culture.

So orature is not peculiar to Africa. We can talk about Asian, African, European, Pacific, and Latin-American oratures. And within each we can talk about classical and contemporary orature. All cultures in the globe have roots in orature. Even their contemporary manifestation in music, literature, plastic arts, and other forms often borrow their images and symbols from the classical past of their orature. The Jungian archetypes are found in myths and stories and when in his life story, Jung says that "what we are to our inward vision . . . can only be expressed by way of myth," or that "myth is more individual and expresses life more precisely than does science," he is only expressing the continuing relevance of orature, some of its aspects at least, even in an age of marvelous science and triumphant technology.[30]

Orature is a living tradition precisely because orality, its base, is always at the cutting edge of the new and the experimental in words and experience. Socrates, the great advocate of orality over writing, was right on the mark in Plato when he said that the written, on the surface at least, stayed the same, a point shared by the advocate of writing over orality, Karen Blixen, when she writes that the greatest wonder about what she had put down for Jogona was that it did not change. Both agree, though the point is positive for Plato and negative for Blixen, that orality does not stand still. What T. S. Eliot wrote in "Burnt Norton," that

> Words strain,
> Crack and sometimes break, under the burden,
> Under the tension, slip, slide, perish,
> Decay with imprecision, will not stay in place,
> Will not stay still,[31]

applies more appropriately to the spoken. But in reality, the two are not divorced. Even setting aside the extension of writing to cover certain signifying systems in orality, there has always been continuous literarization of the oral and oralization of the literary. Word changes and new expressions in orality quickly find themselves in the written and the other way round, though slowly, particularly in the age of the radio and electronic sound systems. Most classic oral stories have now been written down and the next oral narrator may very well have taken the story from the written. When my novel *Devil on the Cross* was first published in Gĩkũyũ in 1982, it was read in groups at homes and factory grounds, on public transport even, the literate becoming the "present" author of the story.

The lines between the written and the orally transmitted are being blurred in the age of the internet and cyberspace. This has been going on for some years with the writing down of the orally transmitted; the electronic transmissions of the written as spoken through the radio and television; or simply the radio as a medium of speech. But it has surely accelerated with all corners of the globe becoming neighborhoods in cyberspace. Through technology, people can speak in real time face to face. The language of texting and emailing and access to everything including pictures and music in real time is producing a phenomenon that is neither pure speech nor pure writing. The language of cyberspace may borrow the language of orality, twitter, chat rooms, we-have-been-talking when they mean we-have-been-texting, or chatting through writing emails, but it is orality mediated by writing. It is neither one nor the other. It's both. It's cyborality.

Will this produce cyborature? Already we have entered the world of e-books and audio books on CDs, a host of endless possibilities. All we can say is that writing and orality are realizing anew the natural alliance they have always had in reality, despite attempts to make the alliance invisible or antagonistic. I hope that this means that no cultures and communities need be denied history because they had not developed a writing system; that the oral and the written are not and have never been real antagonists. Certainly, the powers of their products, orature and literature, will continually be harnessed to enrich creativity in the age of internet and cyberspace. The problem has not been the fact of the oral or the written, but their placement in a hierarchy. Network, not hierarchy, will free the richness of the aesthetic, oral or literary.

An important history of orature is the migration of its main genres across languages, cultures, and territories. The Anansi and Br'er Rabbit migration from West and East Africa to the Caribbean and the Americas or that of the Yoruba deities into Roman Catholic worship in Cuba or Brazil or the vodun from the Fon and Ewe cultures of West Africa into Haiti and now the Americas are recent cases in point. The deities of ancient Egypt were appropriated with new names into Greek mythology and their conception of the universe. A study of orature and its constituent elements and worldview, along with their migratory patterns into new regions and cultures and into different aesthetic genres, should reinforce globalectics and the globalectic reading of texts and the world.

Introduction: Riches of Poor Theory

1. René Wellek and Austin Warren, *Theory of Literature* (San Diego: Harcourt Brace, 1977), 51.

2. Aimé Césaire, *Discourse on Colonialism*, trans. Joan Pinkham (New York: Monthly Review Press, 2000), 33.

3. Edward P. Thompson, *The Poverty of Theory and Other Essays* (New York: Monthly Review Press, 1978), 12.

4. Ibid., 167.

5. Pitika Ntuli and Kwesi Owusu, "A Self Portrait," in *Storms of the Heart: An Anthology of Black Arts & Culture* (London: Camden, 1988), 215.

6. During the tenth Time of the Writer Festival, Natal, March 2007.

7. Jerzy Grotowski, *Towards a Poor Theatre*, trans. Eugenio Barba (London: Eyre Methuen, 1976), 21.

8. See Ngũgĩ wa Thiong'o, *Detained: A Writer's Prison Diary*, African Writer's Series (London: Heinemann, 1981); Ngũgĩ wa Thiong'o, *Decolonising the Mind: The Politics of Language in African Literature* (Oxford: James Currey), 1986; Gicingiri Ndigiriri, *Ngũgĩ wa Thiong'o's Drama and the Kamirithu Popular Experiment* (Trenton, N.J.: Africa World Press, 2007); Ingrid Bjorkmann, *Mother Sing for Me: People's Theater in Kenya* (London: ZED, 1989).

9. L. D. Byam, *Community in Motion: Theatre for Development in Africa*, Critical Studies in Education and Culture Series (Westport, Conn.: Bergin & Garvey), 1999.

10. Christopher Prendergast, ed., *Debating World Literature* (London: Verso, 2004); David Damrosch, *What Is World Literature?* (Princeton, N.J.: Princeton University Press, 2003); David Damrosch, *Teaching World Literature* (New York: Modern Language Association of America, 2009).

11. Georg W. F. Hegel and J. Sibree, *The Philosophy of History* (New York: Dover Publications, 1956).

12. Frantz Fanon, Jean-Paul Sartre, and Constance Farrington, *The Wretched of the Earth* (New York: Grove Press, 1963). See also Albert Memmi, *The Colonizer and the Colonized* (New York: Orion Press, 1965); Dominique O. Mannoni, *Prospero and Caliban: The Psychology of Colonization* (New York: Praeger, 1968).

13. Timothy J. Reiss, *Against Autonomy: Global Dialectics of Cultural Exchange* (Stanford: Stanford University Press, 2002).

14. James Baldwin and Randall Kenan, "Why I Stopped Hating Shakespeare," in *The Cross of Redemption: Uncollected Writings* (New York: Pantheon, 2010), 53.

15. See also my book *Moving the Center: The Struggle for Cultural Freedoms* (Oxford: James Curry, 1993).

1. The English Master and the Colonial Bondsman

1. Messrs. Owuor Anyumba and Taban lo Liyong were then members of African Studies at Nairobi University.

2. See the appendix in Ngũgĩ wa Thiong'o, *Homecoming: Essays in Africa and Caribbean Literature, Culture and Politics* (New York: L. Hill, 1983).

3. Molara Ogundfipe-Leslie, "To a 'Jane Austen' Class at Ibadan University" in *Sew the Old Days and Other Poems* (Ibadan, Nigeria: Evan Brothers [Nigeria Publishers] Limited, 1985), 2–3.

4. Gerald Moore and Ulli Beier, *The Penguin Book of Modern African Poetry* (London: Penguin Books, 1998), 173.

5. In Aimé Césaire, *Discourse on Colonialism*, trans. Joan Pinkham (New York: Monthly Review Press, 2000), 81. Césaire expresses similar sentiments when he says of his 1938 prose poem *Return to My Native Land* that "it was a book in which I tried to gain an understanding of myself. In a certain sense it is closer to the truth than a biography."

6. I have recounted this story in my forthcoming memoir *In the House of the Interpreter.*

7. Césaire, *Discourse on Colonialism*, 43.

8. From Karl Marx's "The Introduction to Contribution to the Critique of Hegel's Philosophy of Right," 1884.

9. Joseph Conrad, *Heart of Darkness and Selected Short Fiction* (New York: Barnes & Noble Classics, 2003), 50.

10. From William Blake, "Auguries of Innocence." Accessed on May 16, 2011, www.online-literature.com/blake/612/.

11. From William Blake, "A Song of Liberty," *The Marriage of Heaven and Hell*. Accessed on May 16, 2011, www.levity.com/alchemy/blake_ma.html.

12. C.L.R. James, *The Black Jacobins: Toussaint L'Ouverture and the San Domingo Revolution*, 2nd rev. ed. (New York: Vintage Books, 1989), 283.

13. Césaire, *Discourse on Colonialism*, 86.

14. Ibid., 91.

15. Aimé Césaire, *Notebook of a Return to My Native Land*, trans. Mirrelle Rosello with Annie Pritchard (Northumberland: Bloodaxe Books, 1995), 127.

16. Franz Fanon, *The Wretched of the Earth*, trans. Constance Farrington (New York: Grove Press, 1963). This same title was released as *The Damned* by *Présence Africaine* in 1963.

17. John H. Smith, "Preface," *The Spirit in the Letter* (Ithaca, N.Y.: Cornell University Press, 1988).

18. Karl Marx, *Capital* (Moscow: Foreign Languages Publishing House, 1954), vol. 1:751.

19. Fanon, *The Wretched of the Earth*, 250.

20. Ngũgĩ wa Thiong'o, *A Grain of Wheat* (William Heinemann, 1967), preface datelined Leeds, November 1966.

2. The Education of the Colonial Bondsman

1. G. W. F. Hegel, *Phenomenology of Spirit*, trans. A. V. Miller (Oxford: Oxford University Press, 1977).

2. It must be remembered that the dialect of master and slave is only a section in a major argument of the entire *Phenomenology of Spirit*.

3. Emmanuel Chukwudi Eze, "The Color of Reason: The Idea of 'Race' in Kanat's Anthology," in *Anthropology and the German Enlightenment*, ed. Katherine Faull (Lewisburg, Penn.: Bucknell University Press, 1995).

4. David Hume, "Of National Characters," in *Essays: Moral, Political, and Literary*, rev. ed., ed. Eugene F. Miller (Indianapolis: Liberty Fund, 1987), 452. http://files.libertyfund.org/files/704/Hume_0059_EBk_v5.pdf.

5. Emmanuel Chukwudi Eze, *Race and the Enlightenment: A Reader* (Cambridge: Blackwell, 1997), 5.

6. Barbara Kirshenblatt-Gimblett, *Destination Culture: Tourism, Museums, and Heritage* (Berkeley: University of California Press, 1998), 34.

7. Patricia Penn Hilden, "Race for Sale: Narratives of Possession in Two 'Ethnic' Museums," *TDR: The Drama Review* 44, no. 3 (Fall 2000): 11–36.

8. Eze, *Race and the Enlightenment*, 6.

9. Frantz Fanon, *The Wretched of the Earth* (New York: Grove Press, 1963), 51.

10. Thomas MaCaulay, "Minutes on Indian Education," in *The Post-Colonial Studies Reader*, ed. Bill Ashcroft, Gareth Griffiths, and Helen Tiffin (London: Routledge, 1995), 428.

11. Samuel Daniel, "Musophilus," in *Selections from the Poetical Works of Samuel Daniel*, ed. John Morris (Bath: Charles Clark, 1855), 148–49.

12. Macaulay, "Minutes," 429.

13. Ibid., 429.

14. Fanon, *The Wretched of the Earth*, 210.

15. Edward Blyden, *Christianity, Islam and the Negro Race* (African Heritage Books I, Edinburgh, [1883] 1972).

16. Blyden quoted in Ngũgĩ wa Thiong'o, *Writers in Politics: Re-engagement with Issues of Literature and Society* (Oxford: James Currey, 1997), 17.

17. Aimé Césaire, Richard Miller, and William Shakespeare, *A Tempest: Based on Shakespeare's The Tempest, Adaptation for a Black Theatre* (New York: TCG Translations, 2002), 61–62.

18. Chinua Achebe, "The Novelist as Teacher," in *Hopes and Impediments: Selected Essays* (New York: Anchor Books, 1990), 43.

19. Ibid., 45.

20. Fanon, *The Wretched of the Earth*, 210.

21. Ibid., 153.

22. Ibid., 166–67.

3. Globalectical Imagination: The World in the Postcolonial

1. This chapter incorporates some features from the 2011 Trilling Lecture that I gave at Columbia University under the same title.

2. Fritz Strich, *Goethe and World Literature*, trans. C. A. M. Sym (London: Routledge, 1949), 35.

3. Johann Peter Eckermann, *Conversations with Goethe* [1835], quoted in David Damrosch, *What Is World Literature?* (Princeton, N.J.: Princeton University Press, 2003), 1.

4. Strich, *Goethe and World Literature*, 350.

5. Adam Smith, *An Inquiry Into the Nature and Causes of the Wealth of Nations*, ed. Edwin Cannan (Library of Economics and Liberty, 1904 edition),

accessed March 7, 2011, www.econlib.org/library/Smith/smWN.html, paragraph IV.7.166.

6. Karl Marx, "Genesis of the Industrial Capitalist," in *Capital*, vol. 1 (1867), accessed March 11, 2011, www.marxists.org/archive/marx/works/1867-c1/ch31.htm.

7. Karl Marx and Frederich Engels, "Bourgeois and Proletarians," in *The Communist Manifesto: A Roadmap to History's Most Important Political Document*, ed. Phil Gasper (Chicago: Haymarket Books, 2005), 44.

8. Ibid.

9. Eckermann, *Conversations with Goethe*; J. E. Spingarn, *Goethe's Literary Essays* (New York: Harcourt, Brace, 1921); Strich, *Goethe and World Literature*; Christopher Prendergast, ed., *Debating World Literature* (London: Verso, 2004); Damrosch, *What Is World Literature?*; David Damrosch, ed., *Teaching World Literature* (New York: Modern Language Association of America, 2009).

10. Richard G. Moulton, *The Ancient Classical Drama: A Study in Literary Evolution Intended for Readers in English and in the Original* (Oxford: Clarendon Press, 1890).

11. Pascale Casanova, *The World Republic of Letters* (Cambridge, Mass.: Harvard University Press, 2007).

12. Timothy J. Reiss, "Perioddity: Considerations on the Geography of Histories," *Modern Language Quarterly* 62 (December 2001): 425–52.

13. Kwame Anthony Appiah, "Is the post- in postmodernism the post- in postcolonial?," *Critical Inquiry* 17 (Winter 1991): 336–57.

14. George D. Thomson, *Aeschylus and Athens* (1973); *Studies in Ancient Greek Society* (London: Lawrence & Wishart, 1954).

15. The bourgeoisie has through its exploitation of the world market given a cosmopolitan character to production and consumption in every country.

16. Frantz Fanon, *The Wretched of the Earth* (New York: Grove Press, 1963), 212.

17. Fredric Jameson, "Third World Literature in the Era of Multinational Capitalism," *Social Text*, no. 15 (Autumn 1986): 68.

18. Damrosch, *What Is World Literature?*, 12.

19. David Damrosch, *Teaching World Literature* (New York: Modern Language Association of America, 2009), 3.

20. Gayatri C. Spivak, *Death of a Discipline* (New York: Columbia University Press, 2003).

21. Erich Auerbach, "Philology and Weltliteratur," trans. Edward and Maire Said, *Centennial Review* 13, no. 1 (1969): 1–17.

22. Edward W. Said, *The World, the Text, and the Critic* (Cambridge, Mass.: Harvard University Press), 1983.

23. Auerbach, "Philology and Weltliteratur," 1–17.

4. The Oral Native and the Writing Master: Orature, Orality, and Cyborality

1. Plato, *Phaedrus*, trans. Christopher Rowe (New York: Penguin Classics, 2005), 63–64.

2. Aristotle, *On Interpretation*, trans. E. M. Edghill, http://classics.mit .edu/Aristotle/interpretation.mb.txt.

3. Where the colonized had a writing system, the colonizer had no problems manufacturing other deficiencies.

4. Isak Dinesen [Karen Blixen], *Out of Africa* (London: Penguin Books, 1954), 115.

5. Claude Lévi-Strauss, *Tristes tropiques* (New York: Penguin Books, 1992), 296.

6. Ibid., 297.

7. Gabriele Schwab, "The Writing Lesson: Imaginary Inscriptions in Cultural Encounters," *Critical Horizons* 4, no. 1 (2003): 55–73.

8. Dinesen, *Out of Africa*, 108.

9. Ibid., 110.

10. Ibid.

11. William Shakespeare, *The Tempest*, act 1, scene 4.

12. Dinesen, *Out of Africa*, 113.

13. Ibid.

14. See his oft-cited book *Oral Tradition as History* (Madison: University of Wisconsin Press, 1985).

15. August 8, 1979. B. A. Ogot, www.unesco.org/culture/africa/html_eng/ projet.htm.

16. As we did not all belong to the English Department, we could not address our concerns within it. Appropriately, we took our case to the Faculty of Arts to which all the humanities belonged.

17. Cynthia Hoehler-Fatton, entry on Anyumba in the *Dictionary of African Biography Project*, edited by Henry Louis Gates Jr. and Emmanuel Akyeampong (Oxford: Oxford University Press, 2011), http://dubois.fas.harvard .edu/DAB. Information also supplied by Dr. Henry Chakava and Chris Wanjala.

18. Ngũgĩ wa Thiong'o, *Homecoming: Essays on African and Caribbean Literature, Culture, and Politics* (Westport, Conn.: Lawrence Hill, 1983), 148.

19. Ibid.

20. Though not embracing the term, many scholars, like Ruth Finnegan, *Oral Literature in Africa* (Oxford: Oxford University Press, 1970); Isidore Okpewho, *African Oral Literature: Backgrounds, Character, and Continuity* (Bloomington: Indiana University Press, 1992); and Leroy Vail and Landeg White, *Power and the Praise Poem: Southern African Voices in History* (Oxford: James Currey, 1992) have done incredible work in this area. Since the changes in university and school curricula in East Africa that included "oral literature," there has been a plethora of scholars and publications on oratures of individual communities. See Wanjikū Kabira, Kavetsa Adagala, and others.

21. See Joseph R. Roach, *Cities of the Dead: Circum-Atlantic Performance* (New York: Columbia University Press, 1996).

22. Ngũgĩ, *Homecoming*, appendix, 147–48.

23. Okabou Ojobolo, and J. P. Clark-Bekederemo, *The Ozidi Saga* (Ibadan: Ibadan University Press, 1977), xxix.

24. Kwesi Owusu, *Storms of the Heart: An Anthology of Black Arts & Culture* (London: Camden, 1988), 215.

25. Ibid., 215.

26. Micere G. Mugo, *African Orature and Human Rights* (Roma: Institute of Southern African Studies, National University of Lesotho, 1991), 12–13.

27. Kamau Brathwaite (MR 1.337–8).

28. Kĩmani Njogu and Rocha Chimerah, *UFUNDISHAJI WA FASIHI* (Nairobi: Jomo Kenyatta Foundation, 1999).

29. From the unpublished manuscript of the play "Mother Sing for Me," by Ngũgĩ wa Thiong'o.

30. C. G. Jung and Aniela Jaffé, *Memories, Dreams, Reflections* (New York: Vintage Books, 1989).

31. T. S. Eliot, "Burnt Norton," part v, www.tristan.icom43.net/quartets/norton.html.

INDEX